C++ Programming Style

Addison-Wesley Professional Computing Series

Brian W. Kernighan, Consulting Editor

C++ Programming Style

Tom Cargill

ADDISON-WESLEY PUBLISHING COMPANY

Reading, Massachusetts   Menlo Park, California   New York   Don Mills, Ontario
Wokingham, England   Amsterdam   Bonn   Sydney   Singapore   Tokyo   Madrid   San Juan
Paris   Seoul   Milan   Mexico City   Taipei

Many of the designations used by manufacturers and sellers to distinguish their products are claimed as trademarks. Where those designations appear in this book and Addison-Wesley was aware of a trademark claim, the designations have been printed in initial capital letters.

The programs and applications presented in this book have been included for their instructional value. They have been tested with care, but are not guaranteed for any particular purpose. The publisher does not offer any warranties or representations, nor does it accept any liabilities with respect to the programs or applications.

The publisher offers discounts on this book when ordered in quantity for special sales. For more information please contact:

Corporate & Professional Publishing Group
Addison-Wesley Publishing Company
One Jacob Way
Reading, Massachusetts 01867

Library of Congress Cataloging-in-Publication Data

Cargill, Tom.
   C++ programming style / Tom Cargill.
      p. cm.
   Includes bibliographical references and index.
   ISBN 0-201-56365-7
   1. C++ (Computer program language) I. Title. II. Title: C plus
   plus programming style.
QA76.73.C153C37 1992   92-15026
005.13'3—dc20   CIP

Cover design by Joyce C. Weston
Text design by Webster Design, Marblehead, MA
Set in 11 point Times by Gex, Inc.

ISBN: 0-201-56365-7
Text printed on recycled and acid-free paper.
5 6 7 8 9 10 11 CRW 97969594
Fifth printing March 1994

Contents

Preface

Almost two decades after the publication of Kernighan and Plauger's classic, *The Elements of Programming Style*, its compact set of rules remains the best general guidance on good programming. Today, however, our programs are larger and our programming languages have changed. We now care as much about how the components of a program fit together as we do about the algorithms and data structures used in each component. DeRemer and Kron coined the terms *programming-in-the-large* and *programming-in-the-small* to make a distinction between the large-scale and small-scale aspects of programs. By programming-in-the-small, they meant dealing with components of a program that are "one to a few pages long" — the size of a typical C++ class. By programming-in-the-large, they meant the structuring of in-the-small components into a program — in C++ terms, dealing with relationships between classes. Kernighan and Plauger concentrated their work on the issues of programming-in-the-small. Their advice about programming-in-the-large is sound, but minimal

> ▶ **Modularize. Use subroutines.**

This book addresses programming style, with more emphasis on programming-in-the-large, and is restricted to the domain of C++ programs. It is written for the programmer who has learned the mechanics of C++, but is experiencing difficulty in applying the language features — particularly the object-oriented features — to programming problems. Though the discussion is limited to C++, many of the observations about programming are true of other languages. I leave the treatment of language-independent style in-the-large to more ambitious authors.

I have adopted Kernighan and Plauger's method of distilling rules of programming style from the critical reading and rewriting of programs. All the programs used here are taken from text books, magazine articles and tutorials on C++ programming. None was created artificially for this work. Some programs are presented exactly as originally published, while others have been altered cosmetically. The alterations range from the correction of in-the-small bugs, which would only distract, to structure-preserving transformations of programs for which copyright was not obtained.

The spirit in which to approach the material is that of an "egoless" code review. We all learn by reading and reviewing each other's programs. The material is not a criticism of individual programmers — it seeks only to differentiate between good and bad programs. No doubt the programs that are presented here as "better" versions have their own shortcomings. The reader is encouraged to examine these programs critically, looking for further improvements in programming style.

Acknowledgments

This book grew from tutorials presented at C++ At Work and various USENIX conferences. My thanks to Rick Friedman of SIGS and John Donnelly and Dan Klein of USENIX for the opportunities to present the material, and to the tutorial participants for their insights. A special word of thanks to the programmers at Solbourne who suffered through the dry run of the first tutorial. Articles written for *The C++ Journal* have also contributed to the book; my thanks to the *Journal's* editor, Livleen Singh. Numerous conversations with Dave Taenzer have influenced my thinking on many topics addressed in the book. Thanks also to John Wait of Addison-Wesley for his confidence and patience.

David Cheriton, James Coggins, Cay Horstmann, David Jordan, Brian Kernighan, Doug Lea, Scott Meyers, Rob Murray, Kathy Stark and Mike Vilot reviewed draft manuscripts, finding many ways to improve the presentation and eliminate bugs. I appreciate all their contributions.

My thanks and love to Carol Meier for her constant support throughout the writing of the book. Between the conception and delivery of this book, we conceived and delivered our first child.

Finally, I wish to acknowledge the following authors and publishers for their kind permission to reproduce material from the following publications:

Davis, S. R. 1991. *Hands-On Turbo C++*. Reading, MA: Addison-Wesley.

Dewhurst, S. C., and Stark, K. T. 1989. *Programming in C++*. Englewood Cliffs, NJ: Prentice Hall.

C++ for C Programmers by Ira Pohl (Redwood City, CA: Benjamin/Cummings Publishing Company,1989) p. 92.

Stroustrup, B. 1991.*The C++ Programming Language,* 2d ed. Reading, MA: Addison-Wesley.

Wiener, R. S., and Pinson, L. J. 1988. *An Introduction to Object-Oriented Programming and C++*. Reading, MA: Addison-Wesley.

Wiener, R. S., and Pinson, L. J. 1990. *The C++ Workbook*. Reading, MA: Addison-Wesley.

Shapiro, J. S. *A C++ Toolkit*. Portions of this work are derived from *A C++ Toolkit*, which is copyright © 1991 by Jonathan S. Shapiro, and are used with permission. A C++ Toolkit is published by Prentice Hall, Inc.

Bibliographic Notes

Kernighan and Plauger [2] remains recommended reading for all programmers. The terms "programming-in-the-large" and "programming-in-the-small" were introduced by DeRemer and Kron [1].

1. DeRemer, F., and Kron, H. "Programming-in-the-large versus Programming-in-the-small," *Proceedings of the International Conference on Reliable Software*, ACM/IEEE, April 1975, Los Angeles, California.

2. Kernighan, B. W., and Plauger, P. J. 1974 (2d ed., 1978). *The Elements of Programming Style*. New York, NY: McGraw-Hill.

Tom Cargill
Boulder, Colorado

0

Introduction

The presentation of material throughout the book follows a uniform method. Each programming style topic is introduced by studying a program — a "style example" — that is flawed in some significant way. The frame of mind in which to approach the programs is that of a peer code review. When reviewing a colleague's code, what are the most important problems to identify and correct? Which parts of the program should be changed to most improve its overall quality? Read and evaluate each program. Form your own opinions about it before reading the commentary and suggested corrections. At the end of each example, return to the original and compare it to the final version of the program; in some cases the accumulated transformations result in a substantial reduction in the size and complexity of the code. Then read the final version critically, with a view to finding further improvements.

Each major lesson learned from studying the programs is captured in a rule of thumb. The nature of the rules varies widely. At one extreme, there are specific, technical rules about avoiding identifiable language pitfalls. At the other extreme are rules that offer guidance on forming abstractions and their relationships in object-oriented programming. All the rules are germane to some aspect of production C++ programming.

It is more important to understand the reasoning behind each rule than to try to adhere blindly to them all. Situations arise in which a programmer should break the rules because a more important goal is achieved. Indeed, some rules are in conflict with others. For example, the rules that urge simplicity are at odds with those that urge completeness. The programmer who not only knows the rule, but also appreciates its rationale, is in a position to judge when it should be broken.

There is a great deal of variety in the programs presented as style examples. This chapter explains some of the decisions that influence how the programs appear.

C++ is an unusual programming language in that it supports programming at so many levels of abstraction of the underlying machine. C++ permits detailed control of computer hardware, almost at the level achieved in an assembly language, yet also accommodates much higher levels of abstraction with classes, inheritance and polymorphism. Among object-oriented languages, C++ is an exception in the degree to which low-level control is left in the programmer's hands.

Many of the ways in which C++ extends C are related to programming-in-the-large. The introduction of member functions, access control, overloading, inheritance and polymorphism reflects a shift towards describing relationships between different components of a program or family of programs, as opposed to coding a single component. Therefore, C++ programming style encompasses in-the-large issues with respect to describing intercomponent relationships. In fact, it becomes difficult to draw the line between programming style and software design. This is natural — C++ programs reflect their design more explicitly than those written in languages like C. Properties of the design can be expressed concretely in the programming language, and C++ programs often tell us a great deal about the underlying design.

I assume a sound reading knowledge of C++ and rarely clarify language detail. Readers should use their preferred primer to review unfamiliar syntax or semantics. Only the more esoteric corners of the language will be explained explicitly, when encountered. For some language details, references to Ellis and Stroustrup are given. These are suggestions for dipping into *The Annotated C++ Reference Manual*, Addison-Wesley, 1990. Typical of a reference manual, Ellis and Stroustrup is hard to digest in large doses; learn to read it selectively to answer specific questions.

Lexical Style

C++ allows many different lexical styles, such as indentation conventions, where to include whitespace, and so on. No preferred lexical style is offered. Most code follows the lexical style of the original program. For example, some programs declare a pointer-to-character as `char* p`; others use `char *p`. Sometimes the null pointer is expressed as `0`, and at other times as `NULL`. Within any example program, a single lexical style is used consistently and followed as the code is modified.

There are two reasons for not adopting a preferred lexical style. First, although lexical style is important in making programs readable, it pales by comparison with issues of programming-in-the-large. For example, whether class declarations should start with public or private member declarations is insignificant compared to whether a program needs one or two classes, and whether or not those classes are related by inheritance. Indeed, lexical details are trivial in the sense that automated tools — pretty-printers of varying degrees of sophistication — can transform any program from one lexical style to another. Discussion of lexical style would detract from the focus of this book.

Second, many issues of lexical style are subjective. For example, redundant parentheses help some programmers, but hinder others. There are programmers who prefer to see a return expression written as `return (x)` while others prefer `return x`. All have the same reason: "It is easier to read." Programmers, as individuals or in teams, must make their own choices on issues of lexical style. In other words, even if I presented my opinions on lexical style, they would be ignored. Perhaps the only objective criterion is that one lexical style should be adopted and used consistently throughout each programming project.

In-line Functions and `const` *Declarations*

Some member functions in sample programs are declared as in-line functions, even though it seems unlikely to help the overall performance of a program using them. Some programmers routinely in-line short member functions by defining their bodies within class declarations, thereby reducing the size of their source text a little. This is usually a mistake. In-line expanded functions usually occupy more code space than the corresponding function calls, especially if in-line functions call other in-line functions. Increased code size due to in-line functions can even *slow* a program by inhibiting the effective operation of code caches. An in-line function should be used in production code only when it provides a demonstrated performance improvement. However, suspect in-line member functions have been left as they appeared in the original code, without comment. There is usually a question of correctness or consistency to address that far outweighs any performance issue. Identification of these spurious in-line functions is left to the reader.

The programs also vary in the degree to which `const` qualifiers are applied to types and member functions. Using `const` carefully throughout a program can permit the compile-time detection of some kinds of errors. Unfortunately, there are different styles in which `const` can be used, and retrofitting `const` to completed programs is notoriously difficult. For these reasons, no attempt has been made to add `const` qualifiers to the programs. The presence or absence of `const` does not affect the overall structure of a program, which is the primary concern.

Virtual Functions

The dynamic binding of virtual functions is a powerful and important part of C++. Yet more of this book is devoted to describing situations in which virtual functions should be removed from programs than to describing situations in which they should be added. The emphasis on the elimination of virtual functions follows directly from observing programs created to demonstrate how to use C++. Example programs where virtual functions are used inappropriately abound; example programs that would be improved by the introduction of virtual functions are rare. I conclude that it is more important to show where to avoid virtual functions than where to use them.

Comments

Most of the programs in this book are sparsely commented. Indeed, they are inadequately commented by typical production programming standards. Additional comments would probably let the reader peruse the programs more quickly, but that would often defeat the purpose of studying the code. With fewer comments the reader is forced to elicit more information directly from the program, requiring more attention to its details. Inferring design decisions by digesting the details is essential to understanding many of the example programs and is a skill worth developing.

Standard I/O versus Streams

Some programs use the standard C I/O library (`printf`, etc.) for formatted character output. Others use the Streams class library (`cout`, etc.). In most cases the programs can be written equally easily and clearly in either form.

Parameterized Types and Exceptions

At the time of writing, parameterized types (templates) had just become available in production C++ compilers, and exception handling remained unavailable. Rather than speculate on the confusion that these language features may cause, it was prudent to wait for their reception by programmers at large and then observe the resulting programs. Only when those programs appear will it be meaningful to offer guidance on avoiding common traps associated with designing programs that use these features.

Exercises

Exercises are offered at the end of most chapters, a few of which involve reading further programs. In some of these exercises, the code exhibits similar flaws to those studied in the chapter. In other exercises, the code demonstrates a well-written program. These exercises are worded not to prejudice the way the reader approaches the code. Try to tackle the code from scratch, as you might in a blind code review.

Program Listings

All the programs shown in the listings throughout the book were mechanically extracted from source files that have been compiled and run on at least one C++ platform. Most programs were run under Cfront 2.0, and a few were run under G++ and Borland C++ 3.0.

Bibliographic Notes

At the time of writing, the definitive description of C++ was Ellis and Stroustrup [1].

1. Ellis, M. A., and Stroustrup, B. 1990. *The Annotated C++ Reference Manual.* Reading, MA: Addison-Wesley.

1

Abstraction

The practice of *abstraction* is central to the creation of software. The single most important abstraction mechanism in C++ is the *class*. A class captures the common properties of the objects instantiated from it; a class characterizes the common behavior of all the objects that are its instances. Identifying appropriate abstractions is a critical part of programming in C++. To find good abstractions, the programmer must understand the underlying properties of the objects manipulated by the program.

To study the class as an abstraction mechanism, we examine a sample program and evaluate its strengths and weaknesses, particularly with respect to the choice of classes. Alternative ways of writing the program with different classes and different class relationships appear. General rules of programming style, which will improve other programs, then emerge from rethinking the design and rewriting the code of the sample program.

Style Example: Pricing Computers

Examine the classes in the program in Listing 1.1. The abstractions in the program are computers, computer components and their prices and rebates. The program determines the price of various configurations of a computer. Two selections must be made when configuring a computer: one for an expansion card and another for a monitor. The slot for an expansion card must contain one of three options: a CD ROM drive, a magnetic tape drive or a network interface; the monitor must be either monochrome or color. In reading the program, think about how it may be simplified. Are the classes providing the right abstractions? Are there ways to eliminate complexity from the program by changing its abstractions?

Listing 1.1 Original program

```
#include <stdio.h>

enum CARD { CDROM, TAPE, NETWORK };
enum MONITOR { MONO, COLOR };

class Card {
public:
virtual int  price() = 0;
virtual char *name() = 0;
virtual int  rebate();
};

class Network : public Card {
public:
    int  price();
    char *name();
};

class CDRom : public Card {
public:
    int  price();
    char *name();
    int  rebate();
};

class Tape : public Card {
public:
    int  price();
    char *name();
};

class Monitor {
public:
virtual int  price() = 0;
virtual char *name() = 0;
};

class Color : public Monitor {
public:
    int  price();
    char *name();
};

class Monochrome : public Monitor {
public:
    int  price();
    char *name();
};
```

```
int Card::rebate()     { return 45; }

int Network::price()  { return 600;          }
char *Network::name() { return "Network"; }

int CDRom::price()     { return 1500;     }
char *CDRom::name()    { return "CDRom"; }
int CDRom::rebate()    { return 135;        }

int Tape::price()      { return 1000;     }
char *Tape::name()     { return "Tape"; }

int Color::price()     { return 1500;     }
char *Color::name()    { return "Color"; }

int Monochrome::price()   { return 500;      }
char *Monochrome::name() { return "Mono"; }

class Computer {
    Card     *card;
    Monitor *mon;
public:
            Computer(CARD, MONITOR);
            ~Computer();
    int     netPrice();
    void    print();
};

int Computer::netPrice()
{
    return mon->price() + card->price()-card->rebate();
}

Computer::Computer(CARD c, MONITOR m)
{
    switch( c ){
    case NETWORK:    card = new Network; break;
    case CDROM:      card = new CDRom;   break;
    case TAPE:       card = new Tape;    break;
    }
    switch( m ){
    case MONO:       mon = new Monochrome; break;
    case COLOR:      mon = new Color;      break;
    }
}
```

```
Computer::~Computer()
{
    delete card;
    delete mon;
}

void Computer::print()
{
    printf("%s %s, net price = %d\n",
        card->name(), mon->name(), netPrice());
}

int main()
{
    Computer mn(NETWORK, MONO);
    Computer mc(CDROM,   MONO);
    Computer mt(TAPE,    MONO);
    Computer cn(NETWORK, COLOR);
    Computer cc(CDROM,   COLOR);
    Computer ct(TAPE,    COLOR);

    mn.print();
    mc.print();
    mt.print();
    cn.print();
    cc.print();
    ct.print();

    return 0;
}
```

The output from the program in Listing 1.1 is

```
Network Mono, net price = 1055
CDRom Mono, net price = 1865
Tape Mono, net price = 1455
Network Color, net price = 2055
CDRom Color, net price = 2865
Tape Color, net price = 2455
```

Each argument to the constructor for class Computer selects an option from a corresponding enumeration:

```
enum CARD { CDROM, TAPE, NETWORK };
enum MONITOR { MONO, COLOR };
```

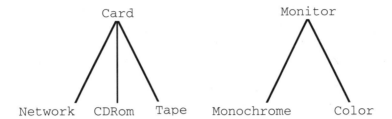

Figure 1.1 `Card` and `Monitor` inheritance hierarchies

The constructor executes a `switch` statement for each argument to create an object of a class corresponding to the argument's value:

```
Computer::Computer(CARD c, MONITOR m)
{
    switch( c ){
    case NETWORK:    card = new Network; break;
    case CDROM:      card = new CDRom;   break;
    case TAPE:       card = new Tape;    break;
    }
    switch( m ){
    case MONO:       mon = new Monochrome; break;
    case COLOR:      mon = new Color;      break;
    }
}
```

The classes form two inheritance hierarchies, one for the choice of card that can occupy the expansion slot and another for the choice of monitor, as shown in Figure 1.1. All inheritance hierarchies in this book are shown with base classes above derived classes.

The base classes, `Card` and `Monitor`, are both abstract classes:

```
class Card {
public:
virtual int  price() = 0;
virtual char *name() = 0;
virtual int  rebate();
};

class Monitor {
public:
virtual int  price() = 0;
virtual char *name() = 0;
};
```

Is the program larger and more elaborate than it needs to be? Is the problem so complex that it requires eight classes, seven of which have virtual functions? Perhaps simpler abstractions can be found that will lead to a simpler program.

Finding a Common Abstraction

The class interfaces of Card and Monitor are similar: Both have price() and name() as pure virtual functions. The difference is that class Card has an additional virtual function, rebate(). Studying the similarities and differences between these classes will clarify their relationships and lead to a better program.

Card and Monitor are similar, but they are not formally related in the inheritance hierarchy. Both Card and Monitor have price() and name() member functions. The classes have member functions with the same names because both classes are computer components. It makes more sense to formalize that common abstraction in a further base class called, say, Component, as shown in Figure 1.2.

Only Card and Monitor change with the introduction of Component. The remainder of the program is unaltered. The new declarations are

```
class Component {
public:
virtual int  price() = 0;
virtual char *name() = 0;
};

class Card : public Component {
public:
virtual int  price() = 0;
virtual char *name() = 0;
virtual int  rebate();
};

class Monitor : public Component {
public:
virtual int  price() = 0;
virtual char *name() = 0;
};
```

Although Component adds another class to the program, it unifies Card and Monitor by identifying a common base abstraction. With the addition of Component, the program better models the problem domain.

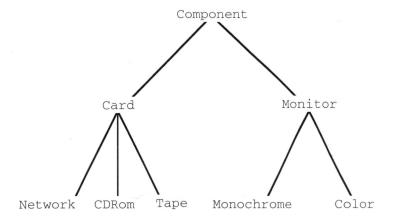

Figure 1.2 Introduction of class `Component`

Should `rebate()` also be a member of `Component`? The classes clearly show that a `Card` object may have a rebate, but a `Monitor` object may not. Is the distinction intrinsic or merely coincidental? The distinction is intrinsic if there is something about monitors, such as government regulation, that prohibits a rebate. In this program the rebate distinction is coincidental: Any component might have a rebate, but no monitors happen to have rebates. With `rebate()` as a member of `Component`, the base classes become

```
class Component {
public:
virtual int  price() = 0;
virtual char *name() = 0;
virtual int  rebate();
};

int Component::rebate()
{
    return 0;
}

class Card : public Component {
public:
virtual int  price() = 0;
virtual char *name() = 0;
virtual int  rebate();
};
```

```
class Monitor : public Component {
public:
virtual int  price() = 0;
virtual char *name() = 0;
};
```

Although `price()` and `name()` are pure virtual functions, `Component::` `rebate()` is not. There is no meaningful default implementation of `price()` and `name()` that the base class might use — that information must be specified by a derived class before an object may be instantiated. In contrast, a rebate of zero is a sound default implementation to use in the base class — the rebate is zero unless the virtual function is overridden in a derived class.

Unification of the base abstractions permits a simplification of `Computer::` `netPrice`. In the original program, the details of `Computer::netPrice` reflect the coincidental difference that `Card` has a rebate, while `Monitor` does not:

```
int Computer::netPrice()
{
    return mon->price() + card->price()-card->rebate();
}
```

The code in the body of `Computer::netPrice` should not depend explicitly on which components have rebates. Instead, it should treat each component uniformly:

```
int Computer::netPrice()
{
    return mon->price()-mon->rebate()
        + card->price()-card->rebate();
}
```

The common computation of `price()-rebate()` for each component suggests another abstraction that belongs in `Component`. If `netPrice()` is added as a member of `Component`, `Computer::netPrice()` would need to call only a single member of `Component`:

```
class Component {
public:
virtual int  price() = 0;
virtual char *name() = 0;
virtual int  rebate();
       int  netPrice();
};
```

```
int Component::netPrice()
{
    return price() - rebate();
}

// ...

int Computer::netPrice()
{
    return mon->netPrice() + card->netPrice();
}
```

Thus far there are three changes to the program. First, a common base class, Component, has been introduced to collect all the component classes into a single inheritance hierarchy. Second, rebate() is a member of Component, making different Component objects behave more uniformly. Elsewhere in the program there is no need to distinguish between components that have rebates and those that do not. Third, adding netPrice() to the Component interface means that clients need not deal with rebates at all. These three changes arise from identifying commonality among classes that may be isolated in a base class. Common properties of the classes have been identified and moved towards the common base class. The general rule is

▶ **Concentrate common abstractions in a base class.**

Differences between Classes

Shifting focus from the *common* properties of the classes, we should also ask: What makes the classes *different*? For example, what is the difference between Network and CDRom? The difference is found in the derived class declarations. Neither class adds new members; they have no additional state nor supplementary behavior. The difference is in their definitions of the virtual functions price(), name() and rebate(). The virtual functions do not vary the *behavior* of the objects of the different derived classes. The only difference between a Network object and a CDRom object is the *values* returned by their virtual functions.

In general, the *behavior* of an object is the way it responds to each stimulus it can receive. Viewing an object in terms of its response to stimuli emphasizes the independence of objects — each object is an autonomous component of a program in execution. The most common form of stimulus is a member function call. The object responds by executing its member function, either to perform a side effect or to return a value, or both. *Polymorphism* — virtual functions — permits objects of different types to respond in different ways to the same stimulus. In this program, the virtual functions do not produce variation in behavior between objects.

The difference between the derived classes can be seen from another perspective. All the information in an object of one of these leaf classes is incorporated in its type. A Tape object, for example, has no data members; every Tape object is equivalent to every other. There is, therefore, no reason to instantiate more than one Tape object, because they must all behave in exactly the same way. Each leaf class is so specialized that its objects cannot be distinguished from one another. Every Tape object is a representative of all Tape objects, leaving little distinction between the Tape class and a Tape object.

Generality is an essential property of programs. Programs and program fragments that address general problems are more useful than those that are restricted to specific problems. This observation is as true of conventional procedural programming as it is of object-oriented programming. Arguments make functions more general and therefore more useful — the function's generalized behavior is converted to a specific behavior by supplying actual argument values when the function is invoked. Similarly, a class is more useful if it describes the properties of many objects, rather than being restricted to one specific object. In practice, a program cannot afford to define a different class for every object that it creates. Rather, each class should characterize a set of objects.

▶   **A class should describe a set of objects.**

Value versus Behavior

The programmer of the original program was drawn into the common trap of thinking that inheritance and virtual functions are the *only* ways to program with C++. The excessive use of inheritance resulted in class declarations in which some classes are so specialized that each describes just one object. Inheritance and polymorphism are powerful tools when behavior varies between objects of different classes. However, in this program the variation is in values, not behavior.

Simple data members and non-virtual functions are sufficient to represent the differences between the component objects. Consider the following Component class for computer components:

```
class Component {
    int    price_;
    char  *name_;
    int    rebate_;
public:
        Component(int p, char *n, int r = 0);
    int   netPrice();
    int   price()    { return price_;  }
    char *name()     { return name_;   }
    int   rebate()   { return rebate_; }
};

Component::Component(int p, char *n, int r)
{
    price_ = p;
    name_ = n;
    rebate_ = r;
}
```

The member functions price(), name() and rebate() are no longer virtual. Each of these member functions is now an in-line access function, delivering the value of a corresponding data member. The difference between components is now a difference in value, not a difference in type. The different values are established by arguments to the constructor.

> ▶ **Use data members for variation in value; reserve virtual**
> **functions for variation in behavior.**

This version of class Component is sufficient to solve the original computer configuration problem. Using a single class, a Component object can be instantiated to describe the name, price and rebate for each of the components. A component with no rebate is modelled by a rebate whose value is zero. A complete program using this version of Component is shown in Listing 1.2. Note that Network, CDRom, Tape, Color and Monochrome are objects, not classes. Class Component defines the objects' general properties, and each object carries specific information about the component that it describes. Class Computer has a corresponding change: It no longer creates and destroys objects.

Listing 1.2 Components described by objects

```
#include <stdio.h>

enum CARD { CDROM, TAPE, NETWORK };
enum MONITOR { MONO, COLOR };

class Component {
    int   price_;
    char *name_;
    int   rebate_;
public:
        Component(int p, char *n, int r = 0);
    int   netPrice();
    int   price()     { return price_;  }
    char *name()      { return name_;   }
    int   rebate()    { return rebate_; }
};

Component::Component(int p, char *n, int r)
{
    price_ = p;
    name_ = n;
    rebate_ = r;
}

int Component::netPrice()
{
    return price_ - rebate_;
}

Component Network(600, "Network", 45);

Component CDRom(1500, "CDRom", 135);

Component Tape(1000, "Tape", 45);

Component Color(1500, "Color");

Component Monochrome(500, "Mono");

class Computer {
    Component   *card;
    Component   *mon;
public:
        Computer(CARD, MONITOR);
    int     netPrice();
    void    print();
};
```

```
int Computer::netPrice()
{
    return mon->netPrice() + card->netPrice();
}

Computer::Computer(CARD c, MONITOR m)
{
    switch( c ){
    case NETWORK:    card = &Network;   break;
    case CDROM:      card = &CDRom;     break;
    case TAPE:       card = &Tape;      break;
    }
    switch( m ){
    case MONO:       mon = &Monochrome; break;
    case COLOR:      mon = &Color;      break;
    }
}

void Computer::print()
{
    printf("%s %s, net price = %d\n",
        card->name(), mon->name(), netPrice());
}

int main()
{
    Computer mn(NETWORK, MONO);
    Computer mc(CDROM,   MONO);
    Computer mt(TAPE,    MONO);
    Computer cn(NETWORK, COLOR);
    Computer cc(CDROM,   COLOR);
    Computer ct(TAPE,    COLOR);

    mn.print();
    mc.print();
    mt.print();
    cn.print();
    cc.print();
    ct.print();

    return 0;
}
```

Reintroducing Inheritance

In one respect, the program has lost ground in the transformation. The original program specified only once, in `Card::rebate()`, that the default rebate for cards is 45. With the current definition of `Component`, the values of all non-zero rebates must be specified in the object declarations. The program has no place to record a default rebate specifically for cards. The program does need to distinguish cards from monitors. Inheritance can provide appropriate specialization with distinct constructors for cards and monitors. We must reintroduce the classes Card and Monitor to provide constructors with the appropriate rebate defaults. The inheritance hierarchy is shown in Figure 1.3.

The specialization in the derived classes is limited to their constructors. The default rebates are specified as default argument values to the constructors for Card and Monitor.

```
class Card : public Component {
public:
    Card(int p, char *n, int r = 45) : Component(p, n, r) {}
};

class Monitor : public Component {
public:
    Monitor(int p, char *n, int r = 0) : Component(p, n, r) {}
};
```

Generally, public inheritance is used when the derived class is a specialization of the base class, that is, when the classes exhibit the "is a kind of" relationship. A Card *is a kind of* Component; a Monitor *is a kind of* Component. In this case, the specialization applies only during construction — once constructed, all component objects behave uniformly. Limiting the variation in the derived classes to initialization — *constructor specialization* — is a legitimate use of inheritance.

▶ **A public derived class should be a specialization of its base class.**

It is interesting to note that Card and Monitor now differ in a *default value*, implemented as a constructor default argument value. In the original version of the program, Card and Monitor differed in a *default behavior*, implemented as a virtual function.

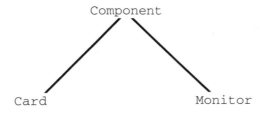

Figure 1.3 Inheritance reintroduced

Removing the Enumerations

In place of five `Component` objects, there are now three `Card` objects and two `Monitor` objects. Only one rebate value need be specified; only the `CDRom` object deviates from its default.

```
Card Network(600, "Network");

Card CDRom(1500, "CDRom", 135);

Card Tape(1000, "Tape");

Monitor Color(1500, "Color");

Monitor Monochrome(500, "Mono");
```

The reintroduction of `Card` and `Monitor` can simplify the program in another way. The arguments to `Computer::Computer` specify one `CARD` and one `MONITOR` value. The enumerations place a level of indirection between the constructor and the information it needs, without adding any flexibility. The constructor really needs the `Component` objects and has to map each enumeration value to an object. Maintaining this mapping is complicated. For example, to add another `Monitor`, say, `GreyScale`, the programmer has to (1) add `GREY_SCALE` to the `MONITOR` enumeration type, (2) declare a `GreyScale` object, and (3) add a `GREY_SCALE` case to the constructor's `switch` statement on its `MONITOR` argument. Eliminating the enumerations and dealing directly with objects is much simpler.

`Card` and `Monitor` are distinct types. If `Computer::Computer` takes pointers to objects as its arguments, the enumerations and the `switch` statements can be removed. The constructor then directly receives the information it requires; there is no need for the mapping from enumeration to object. Without the mapping, a component can be added by simply declaring another object. For this transformation, `CARD` and `MONITOR` are removed, and the constructor for `Computer` becomes

```
Computer::Computer(Card *c, Monitor *m)
{
    card = c;
    mon = m;
}
```

Since one argument is of type pointer-to-Card and the other is a pointer-to-Monitor, a Computer can still only be constructed with exactly one card and one monitor. Listing 1.3 shows the whole of this version of the program.

Compare the size of the program in Listing 1.3 with that of Listing 1.1; the final code is about half the size of the original. Smaller programs are usually easier to read and modify than larger ones. For this program, better abstractions have both improved its architecture and reduced its size. Reduced code size itself was not the goal; expressing a program in the fewest possible lines of code rarely results in a good solution. But better designs often require less code than poorer ones, because the better designs use the right abstractions.

Listing 1.3 Constructor specialization

```
#include <stdio.h>

class Component {
    int   price_;
    char *name_;
    int   rebate_;
public:
        Component(int p, char *n, int r = 0);
    int   netPrice();
    int   price()     { return price_;  }
    char *name()      { return name_;   }
    int   rebate()    { return rebate_; }
};

Component::Component(int p, char *n, int r)
{
    price_ = p;
    name_ = n;
    rebate_ = r;
}

int Component::netPrice()
{
    return price_ - rebate_;
}

class Card : public Component {
public:
    Card(int p, char *n, int r = 45) : Component(p, n, r) {}
};
```

```
class Monitor : public Component {
public:
    Monitor(int p, char *n, int r = 0) : Component(p, n, r) {}
};

Card Network(600, "Network");

Card CDRom(1500, "CDRom", 135);

Card Tape(1000, "Tape");

Monitor Color(1500, "Color");

Monitor Monochrome(500, "Mono");

class Computer {
    Card    *card;
    Monitor *mon;
public:
            Computer(Card *, Monitor*);
    int     netPrice();
    void    print();
};

int Computer::netPrice()
{
    return mon->netPrice() + card->netPrice();
}

Computer::Computer(Card *c, Monitor *m)
{
    card = c;
    mon = m;
}

void Computer::print()
{
    printf("%s %s, net price = %d\n",
        card->name(), mon->name(), netPrice());
}
```

```
int main()
{
    Computer mn(&Network,  &Monochrome);
    Computer mc(&CDRom,     &Monochrome);
    Computer mt(&Tape,      &Monochrome);
    Computer cn(&Network,   &Color);
    Computer cc(&CDRom,     &Color);
    Computer ct(&Tape,      &Color);

    mn.print();
    mc.print();
    mt.print();
    cn.print();
    cc.print();
    ct.print();

    return 0;
}
```

Summary

Both the original and the final versions of the program provide default rebates. The version in Listing 1.1 uses the default behavior of virtual functions in base classes. The version in Listing 1.3 uses default argument values in derived constructors. Since a rebate is a value, it is represented more directly by a data member.

Both major flaws in the original program were related to inheritance. The first flaw was overspecialization — making classes so specific that each described only one object. A class should describe the common properties of a set of objects, not just a single object. The second major flaw was the use of virtual functions to represent variation of a value. Variation in value can be programmed more easily with data members than with virtual functions. A simpler inheritance hierarchy, with a common base abstraction for all objects, formed a more accurate model.

The power and novelty of inheritance and virtual functions tempt programmers to use them at every opportunity. Not every programming problem requires the muscle of virtual functions. There is nothing wrong with using simple data members to represent values that distinguish objects. Programmers should not reject standard, reliable programming techniques merely because C++ offers more sophisticated techniques.

▶ **Polymorphism is not the solution to every programming problem.**

Bibliographic Notes

Abstraction is a central thread of Booch [1]. See also the first chapter of both Budd [2] and Wirfs-Brock *et al.* [6]. The treatment of "data abstraction" and "abstract data types" in [3], [4] and [5] is also of interest.

1. Booch, G. 1990. *Object-Oriented Design with Applications.* Redwood City, CA: Benjamin/Cummings.

2. Budd, T. 1991. *An Introduction to Object-Oriented Programming.* Reading, MA: Addison-Wesley.

3. Cox, B. J., and Novobilski, A. J. 1991. *Object-Oriented Programming: An Evolutionary Approach*, 2d ed. Reading, MA: Addison Wesley.

4. Gorlen, K. E., Orlow, S. M., and Plexico, P. S. 1990. *Data Abstraction and Object-Oriented Programming in C++.* Chichester, England: Wiley.

5. Meyer, B. 1988. *Object-Oriented Software Construction.* Englewood Cliffs, NJ: Prentice-Hall.

6. Wirfs-Brock, R., Wilkerson, B., and Wiener, L. 1990. *Designing Object-Oriented Software.* Englewood Cliffs, NJ: Prentice-Hall.

Exercise

1.1. Study the classes in Listing 1.4. The `main()` function generates the following output:

```
The atomic weight: 196.9665
The atomic number: 79
Price per ounce: 450.75
```

Evaluate the abstractions and the corresponding classes in this program, applying the criteria established in this chapter. (The identifiers `Pb` and `Au` are the chemical symbols for the elements lead and gold, from the Latin *plumbum* and *aurum*, respectively.)

Listing 1.4 Classes Pb and Au

```
#include <iostream.h>

class Pb
{
private:
 unsigned atomicNumber;
 float atomicWeight;
 float pricePerOunce;

public:
 Pb(void)
  {
   atomicNumber = 82;
   atomicWeight = 207.2;
   pricePerOunce = 0.01;
  }

 unsigned getNumber(void) { return atomicNumber; }

 float getWeight(void) { return atomicWeight; }

 float getPrice(void) { return pricePerOunce; }

 void output(void)
  {
   cout << "The atomic weight: " << atomicWeight << "\n";
   cout << "The atomic number: " << atomicNumber << "\n";
   cout << "Price per ounce: " << pricePerOunce << "\n\n";
  }
};

class Au
{
private:
 unsigned atomicNumber;
 float atomicWeight;
 float pricePerOunce;

public:
 Au(void)
  {
   atomicNumber = 79;
   atomicWeight = 196.9665;
   pricePerOunce = 450.75;
  }
```

```
 Au(Pb& lead)
 {
  atomicWeight = lead.getWeight() - 10.2335;
  atomicNumber = lead.getNumber() - 3;
  pricePerOunce = lead.getPrice() + 450.74;
 }

 void output(void)
 {
  cout << "The atomic weight: " << atomicWeight << "\n";
  cout << "The atomic number: " << atomicNumber << "\n";
  cout << "Price per ounce: " << pricePerOunce << "\n\n";
 }
};

main()
{
 Pb myLead;

 Au myGold = myLead;

 myGold.output();
}
```

2

Consistency

There are two principal views of a class: its *interface* and its *implementation.* The interface, defined by the public members of the class, determines the services that each object of the class provides to clients elsewhere in the program. The implementation, which is usually encapsulated as private members and inaccessible to the clients, realizes these services. A programmer must consider both views when creating a class. The interface must present a coherent abstraction. The implementation must yield objects that behave consistently with the abstraction. This chapter examines issues of consistency with respect to interface and implementation.

At any time, each object is in some *state* determined by the collective values of its data members. The state can be critical to understanding the object, whether viewed externally, through its interface, or internally, with respect to its implementation. Through the interface, the object is driven from state to state to meet its clients' needs. For example, by storing information in a table object, a client deliberately changes the state of the table, making it suitable for subsequent retrieval operations. The implementation must maintain the table object's state such that clients receive the correct answers from retrieval operations.

The interface and implementation may use different models of an object's state, known as the *logical state* and *physical state*, respectively. The logical state model is usually a simplification of the physical state model, in which more than one physical state corresponds to a single logical state. For example, if the table object caches the results of recent retrievals as an optimization, the physical state includes the cache, but the cache is not visible through the public interface; the cache is not part of the logical state.

Style Example: Class `string`

Examine class `string` in Listing 2.1. Concentrate on the state of `string` objects and the consistency of the interface and implementation of the `string` class. Look for inconsistencies in the class definition. The code raises many issues; do not stop after encountering the first inconsistency.

Listing 2.1 Original Class `string`

```cpp
#include <string.h>
#include <iostream.h>

class string {
    char* s;
    int   len;
public:
    string() { s = new char[80]; len = 80; }
    string(int n) { s = new char[n]; len = n; }
    string(char* p) { len = strlen(p);
                      s = new char[len + 1];
                      strcpy(s, p); }
    string(string& str);
    ~string() { delete [] s; }
    void assign(char* str) { strcpy(s, str);
                             len = strlen(str); }
    void print() { cout << s << "\n"; }
    void concat(string& a, string& b);
};

string::string(string& str)
{
    len = str.len;
    s = new char[len];
    strcpy(s, str.s);
}

void string::concat(string& a, string& b)
{
    len = a.len + b.len;
    s = new char[len];
    strcpy(s, a.s);
    strcat(s, b.s);
}
```

The representation of a `string` object is a pointer-to-character, s, and an integer length, `len`. Class `string` has four constructors, a destructor and three other member functions: `assign()`, `print()` and `concat()`. The following code fragment uses five instances of class `string`:

```
char* str = "The wheel that squeaks the loudest\n";
string a(str), b, author("Josh Billings\n"), both, quote;

b.assign("Is the one that gets the grease\n");
both.concat(a, b);
quote.concat(both, author);
quote.print();
```

The output is:

```
The wheel that squeaks the loudest
Is the one that gets the grease
Josh Billings
```

Well-defined State

The first two constructors share a common problem.

```
string() { s = new char[80]; len = 80; }
string(int n) { s = new char[n]; len = n; }
```

If either of these constructors is used, the initial state of the `string` object will be undefined. The following code attempts to display two strings, one constructed by each of the first two constructors.

```
string x, y(128);
x.print();
y.print();
```

For both x and y, the result of calling `print()` is undefined because the contents of the freshly allocated character array that x.s or y.s points to are undefined. These constructors allocate memory, but do not initialize it. The stream output object, `cout`, simply writes out characters until it encounters the first null byte (`'\0'`), wherever it appears in memory.

The purpose of a constructor is to initialize its object. The very least that a constructor should do is to place the object in a well-defined state.

> ▶ **A constructor should put its object in a well-defined state.**

A safe choice of initial state for the first two `string` constructors is the empty string; `s[0]` should be set to a null byte.

Another improvement, although of less importance, should also be made to the first two constructors. These constructors are almost identical: Each allocates an array of characters, saves the pointer in `s` and records the size of the array in `len`. The only difference between them is that one uses a default value for the array size and the other takes an argument to specify the size. In other respects the functions are the same. It would be better to use one constructor with a default argument. The following single constructor replaces both constructors, correcting both problems encountered so far:

```
string(int n = 80) { s = new char[n];
                     s[0] = '\0';
                     len = n; }
```

In general, replacing function overloading by a default argument makes a program easier to maintain because there is only one copy of the function body. In this program the overloaded functions are constructors. The same principle applies to other member and nonmember functions.

> ▶ **Consider default arguments as an alternative to function overloading.**

Consistent Physical State

The third `string` constructor makes a copy of its character string argument. This constructor does initialize `s`, putting the `string` object in a well-defined state, but its treatment of `len` is inconsistent with the first two constructors. The first two constructors set `len` to the size of the allocated character array. The third constructor sets `len` to the length of the string — one less than the size of the array. Is `len` the size of the dynamic array or the length of the string stored in the array? Either would make sense, but all the constructors and other member functions must agree on the representation of the string. Member functions cannot interpret the state of a string object consistently unless `len` has a single meaning.

The bug could be in either the first two constructors or the third constructor. The way in which the last constructor and the `assign()` and `concat()` member functions use `len` may indicate whether `len` is really the array size or the length of the string. Let us examine all three in turn. First, the copy constructor uses `len` as the size of the array:

```
string::string(string& str)
{
    len = str.len;
    s = new char[len];
    strcpy(s, str.s);
}
```

The copy constructor suggests the bug is in the constructor that takes a pointer-to-`char` argument. Second, the `assign()` member function sets `len` to the string length, suggesting the bug is in the first two constructors:

```
void assign(char* str) { strcpy(s, str);
                         len = strlen(str); }
```

Third, the `concat()` member function only makes matters worse by using `len` in neither of the ways established by the other member functions:

```
void string::concat(string& a, string& b)
{
    len = a.len + b.len;
    s = new char[len];
    strcpy(s, a.s);
    strcat(s, b.s);
}
```

On the one hand, if `len` is the array size, the array allocated by `concat()` is too large by one element. On the other hand, if `len` is the length of the string, the allocated array is too small by one element. Under either interpretation of `len`, there is an off-by-one error in the size of the array allocated by `concat()`. Probably, the programmer could not decide how to use `len`, vacillated, and thus failed to resolve the question. The state of a `string` object has no consistent interpretation of its data member `len` in the original program.

Class Invariants

For each class it should be possible to write a set of *class invariant* conditions that are true throughout the lifetime of every object of the class. For example, if `len` is to be the string length, a class invariant of `string` is

```
len == strlen(s)
```

A class invariant is similar to a loop invariant. A loop invariant holds at the beginning of a loop; each iteration of the loop preserves the invariant; and, therefore, the invariant must hold at the end of the loop. Class invariants hold for the lifetime of each object of the class. Constructors establish the class invariants, and then other member functions preserve the invariants so that they hold throughout the lifetime of the object.

▶ **Define object states consistently — identify class invariants.**

Some programming languages, such as Eiffel, provide explicit language mechanisms for expressing and checking class invariants. C++ provides no formal support; the programmer decides how to apply class invariants. In this respect, class invariants are again similar to loop invariants. With a loop invariant in mind, a C++ programmer has two options when coding a loop. Having written the loop, the programmer may add the invariant as a comment or formally incorporate it in the code as an assertion. (Assertions are easy to add with the `assert` macro defined in the standard header file `assert.h`.) Commenting a class invariant is as easy as commenting a loop invariant, but incorporating a class invariant as an assertion in the code is harder. There is no single place in the source code of a class to put class invariant assertions. Since every member function must preserve the class invariants, the assertion must be tested in every member function that alters its object's state. One approach is to collect all the class invariant assertions in a special member function that is called from the beginning or end (or both) of every member function. Few C++ programmers go to this much trouble; commenting class invariants is more common, though not as common as it might be.

A version of class `string` in which `len` consistently has the value of `strlen(s)` is shown in Listing 2.2. A comment in the class declaration documents the class invariant for `len`. Each member function respects the invariant.

Listing 2.2 `string` with consistent `len`

```
#include <string.h>
#include <iostream.h>

class string {
    char* s;
    int    len;       // len == strlen(s)
public:
    string(int n = 80) { s = new char[n];
                         s[0] = '\0';
                         len = 0; }
    string(char* p) { len = strlen(p);
                      s = new char[len + 1];
                      strcpy(s, p); }
    string(string& str);
    ~string() { delete [] s; }
    void assign(char* str) { strcpy(s, str);
                             len = strlen(str); }
    void print() { cout << s << "\n"; }
    void concat(string& a, string& b);
};

string::string(string& str)
{
    len = str.len;
    s = new char[len+1];
    strcpy(s, str.s);
}

void string::concat(string& a, string& b)
{
    len = a.len + b.len;
    s = new char[len+1];
    strcpy(s, a.s);
    strcat(s, b.s);
}
```

Consistent Use of Dynamic Memory

The version of `string` in Listing 2.2 still contains some bugs and inconsistencies. The inconsistencies in the management of dynamic memory are as serious as the inconsistencies already discovered. There are two questions to ask about all dynamically allocated memory: First, is the dynamic memory large enough to hold the information to be stored in it? Second, is all the dynamic memory recovered?

The array of characters allocated by the default constructor is certainly large enough to hold the empty string:

```
string(int n = 80) { s = new char[n];
                     s[0] = '\0';
                     len = 0; }
```

The underlying assumption in this constructor is that the memory for the string is allocated at object creation and must be large enough for any character string that the object might have to hold during its lifetime. The `assign()` member function is consistent with this assumption:

```
void assign(char* str) { strcpy(s, str);
                         len = strlen(str); }
```

The `strcpy()` call in `assign()` simply copies the argument string without regard for its length or the size of the target character array. The client programmer must ensure — no matter which constructor is used — that the size of the array left by the constructor is large enough for any string copied in by `assign()`.

The `concat()` member function takes a different approach: It always determines dynamically the exact size of the array needed for each string that it builds. The character array that is already allocated by the `string` object is ignored by `concat()`, even if it is sufficiently large:

```
void string::concat(string& a, string& b)
{
    len = a.len + b.len;
    s = new char[len+1];
    strcpy(s, a.s);
    strcat(s, b.s);
}
```

There is an inconsistency in the way `assign()` and `concat()` behave. They differ over whether or not to dynamically allocate a character array for the new value of the `string` object: `assign()` never does; `concat()` always does.

Interface Consistency

Which approach to controlling the array size is better? Like many software decisions, neither approach is intrinsically "right" nor "wrong." There are advantages to both techniques. Leaving the array as allocated during construction (as `assign()` does) is efficient, since there are no further calls to the memory allocator. Dynamically determining the array size for each string (as concat() does) is safer, since there is no opportunity for "wild writes" off the end of the array.

Either approach might be used, but the class should consistently follow one or the other, not use a mixture of both. A programmer trying to use the class has to learn that different conventions apply for different operations in the interface. The programmer who has used only concat(), and knows that the representation grows dynamically, will expect the same behavior of assign() and will be understandably upset when assign() writes to memory beyond the end of the array.

▶ **Define a class interface consistently — avoid surprises.**

Deallocating Dynamic Memory

There is a second problem with respect to managing dynamic memory in class string: a "memory leak," which occurs when not all of the memory allocated through new is released by delete. The leak is not in the constructors nor destructor. Each constructor executes new exactly once, obtains a pointer to an array of characters and saves the pointer in s. A string object always has an array for storing its string, and that memory is released at the end of the object's lifetime by the delete [] s in the destructor.

The memory leak is in concat() because it allocates a new array without disposing of the current one. When concat() executes

```
s = new char[len+1];
```

s is immediately overwritten by a new pointer value. The previous pointer is lost, making the character array to which it pointed a block of garbage memory.

To correct the memory leak, concat() must ensure that the old array is deleted. Every use of new creates a dynamic object (or, as in this case, a dynamic array of objects). It is critical to establish an "owner" for each dynamic object — the owner is the object that takes responsibility for destroying the dynamic object when it is no longer needed. The simplest ownership policy is that the object that executes the new owns the dynamic object and must destroy it. Under this policy, class string must delete all the character arrays allocated by its constructors and other member functions.

▶ **Identify the** delete **for every** new.

For concat(), the solution is not as simple as adding a delete [] s before the new is executed. The following code *does not* adequately solve the problem:

```
void string::concat(string& a, string& b)
{
    len = a.len + b.len;
    delete [] s;
    s = new char[len+1];
    strcpy(s, a.s);
    strcat(s, b.s);
}
```

What is wrong with this version of concat()? Suppose x and y are instances of string, and concat() is called from the expression x.concat(y, x). Inside concat(), the string object x can be accessed by means of two aliases: The this pointer and the argument b both refer to x. As concat() executes, the character array to which x.s pointed is deleted through one of the aliases, this->s, *before* being passed to strcpy() as the other alias, b.s. By the time strcpy() executes, the character array has already been deallocated, possibly even reallocated, by the new in concat().

The memory leak in concat() must be corrected by adding a delete that is applied only after the new string has been built:

```
void string::concat(string& a, string& b)
{
    len = a.len + b.len;
    char* new_s = new char[len+1];
    strcpy(new_s, a.s);
    strcat(new_s, b.s);
    delete [] s;
    s = new_s;
}
```

Style Example: A Second Approach

Rather than correct all the remaining problems in class string, we transfer our attention to a different string class, in which most of these problems have been avoided. Examine class SimpleString in Listing 2.3. Although class SimpleString is an improvement over class string, SimpleString has some defects.

Listing 2.3 Original class `SimpleString`

```cpp
#include <string.h>

class SimpleString {
    char *_string;
    int _length;
public:
    SimpleString();
    SimpleString(const char*);
    SimpleString(SimpleString& s);
    ~SimpleString();

    const char *string() const;
    SimpleString& operator=(const char *);
    SimpleString& operator=(const SimpleString&);
};

char *
Strdup(const char *s)
{
    char *s2 = new char[strlen(s) + 1];
    strcpy(s2, s);

    return s2;
}

SimpleString::SimpleString()
{
    _string = 0;
    _length = 0;
}

SimpleString::~SimpleString()
{
    delete [] _string;
}

SimpleString::SimpleString(SimpleString& s)
{
    if (s._string) {
        _string = Strdup(s._string);
        _length = s._length;
    }
    else {
        _string = 0;
        _length = 0;
    }
}
```

```
SimpleString::SimpleString(const char *s)
{
    _string = s ? Strdup(s) : 0;
    _length = s ? strlen(s) : 0;
}

const char *
SimpleString::string()
const
{
    return _string;
}

SimpleString&
SimpleString::operator=(const char *s)
{
    delete [] _string;
    _string = s ? Strdup(s) : 0;
    _length = s ? strlen(s) : 0;
    return *this;
}

SimpleString&
SimpleString::operator=(const SimpleString& s)
{
    delete [] _string;
    _string = s._string ? Strdup(s._string) : 0;
    _length = _string ? s._length : 0;
    return *this;
}
```

Like class `string`, class `SimpleString` represents a character string by a pointer-to-character, `_string`, and an integer, `_length`. The `_length` member is always the length of the character string, if there is one. A `SimpleString` may have no string at all, represented by a null pointer-to-character and a zero length. In `SimpleString`, there are no off-by-one errors, memory leaks, nor inconsistencies in the representation or interface. Still, `SimpleString` has some shortcomings.

Redundancy

The `_length` member of `SimpleString` consistently records the length of the string. A class invariant for `_length` must cover two cases: If `_string` is not a null pointer, then `_length` is the string length; if `_string` is a null pointer, then `_length` is zero.

```
( _string
    ? _length == strlen(_string)
    : _length == 0 )
```

The value of _length is computed correctly after each change of state in a SimpleString object. However, the length information is never used. Everywhere that SimpleString needs to know the length of a string, the value is recomputed from scratch within Strdup(). For example, the copy constructor copies the value of _length from its argument, but still calls strlen() from Strdup() to compute the length of the string.

About one quarter of the implementation of SimpleString is required to maintain the correct value of _length. The code should not be in the class if it is not serving a useful purpose. SimpleString is improved by eliminating _length.

▶ **Avoid computing and storing state information that is never used.**

The situation would be different if SimpleString made use of _length in order to avoid recomputing its string's length. Though redundant from an information-theoretic point of view, _length would then be serving a useful purpose by making SimpleString faster. The rule above should not be interpreted as "save as little information as possible." Rather, it means that information should be saved only if it is to be used later.

Dynamic Memory and `operator=`

Class SimpleString defines two assignment operators:

```
SimpleString&
SimpleString::operator=(const char *s)
{
    delete [] _string;
    _string = s ? Strdup(s) : 0;
    _length = s ? strlen(s) : 0;
    return *this;
}
```

```
SimpleString&
SimpleString::operator=(const SimpleString& s)
{
    delete [] _string;
    _string = s._string ? Strdup(s._string) : 0;
    _length = _string ? s._length : 0;
    return *this;
}
```

Although there is no memory leak in the class, both operator functions may `delete` memory prematurely. We saw in `string::concat()` that care is needed in timing the deletion of dynamic memory. If `operator=(const SimpleString&)` is invoked from an expression in which both sides of an assignment refer to the same `SimpleString` object, the results will be undefined. Though it is unlikely that a programmer would write `x=x` explicitly, the assignment may arise indirectly. If `a` and `b` are references to `SimpleString` that happen to refer to the same object, then `a=b` is effectively `x=x`. No matter how the situation arises, if `operator=` is invoked with an argument that refers to `this`, the old string is deleted before being passed as the argument to `Strdup()`, giving undefined results. The correction is to compare the argument against the value of `this`, and do nothing if they are equal.

```
SimpleString&
SimpleString::operator=(const SimpleString& s)
{
    if( this == &s )
        return *this;
    delete [] _string;
    _string = s._string ? Strdup(s._string) : 0;
    _length = _string ? s._length : 0;
    return *this;
}
```

▶ **When defining** `operator=`, **remember** `x = x`.

For the `delete` problem to arise with `operator=(const char*)`, the assignment must be `x=x.string()`, or the equivalent disguised as `a=b.string()`. The assignment could also occur as `x=s`, where s is a pointer to constant character whose value is `x.string()`. Again, no matter how the situation arises, if `operator=` is invoked with a pointer argument that corresponds to the string to be deleted, the results of calling `Strdup()` will be undefined. As with `string::concat()`, the solution is to defer the `delete` until the character string has been copied.

```
SimpleString&
SimpleString::operator=(const char *s)
{
    char* prev_string = _string;
    _string = s ? Strdup(s) : 0;
    _length = s ? strlen(s) : 0;
    delete [] prev_string;
    return *this;
}
```

Note the similarities in the bodies of the operator functions. Both make a copy of a string and delete the old string. Instead of performing the same work in two different places, one operator function could call the other. As with the two constructors in class `string` that collapsed to a single constructor with a default argument, there is no reason to maintain two copies of the same code.

One Last Detail

The last improvement to `SimpleString` involves the utility function `Strdup()`, which makes a copy of a character string in a freshly allocated block of memory. The problem with `Strdup()` is not one of consistency, but simply that everywhere that `Strdup()` is called in `SimpleString`, the code in the calling context follows a pattern. Before each call there is a test to ensure that the argument pointer is non-null. On return from each call to `Strdup()`, the result is always stored in `_string`. The implementation of the class is simplified when `Strdup()` is replaced by a private member function that tests the pointer, makes a copy of the string and then saves the new pointer in `_string`. This change merely eliminates repeated code by placing it in a common subroutine. We apply a rule from Kernighan and Plauger [p. 15]:

> ▶ **Replace repetitive expressions by calls to a common function.**

Listing 2.4 shows `SimpleString` rewritten to incorporate this and the other improvements.

Listing 2.4 `SimpleString` rewritten

```
#include <string.h>
```

```
class SimpleString {
    char *_string;
    void duplicate(const char *);
public:
    SimpleString();
    SimpleString(const char *);
    SimpleString::SimpleString(SimpleString&);
    ~SimpleString();

    const char *string() const;
    SimpleString& operator=(const char *);
    SimpleString& operator=(const SimpleString&);
};

void
SimpleString::duplicate(const char *s)
{
    if( s ) {
        _string = new char[strlen(s) + 1];
        strcpy(_string, s);
    }
    else
        _string = 0;
}

SimpleString::SimpleString()
{
    _string = 0;
}

SimpleString::~SimpleString()
{
    delete [] _string;
}

SimpleString::SimpleString(SimpleString& s)
{
    duplicate(s._string);
}

SimpleString::SimpleString(const char *s)
{
    duplicate(s);
}

const char *
SimpleString::string()
const
{
    return _string;
}
```

```
SimpleString&
SimpleString::operator=(const char *s)
{
    char *prev_string = _string;
    duplicate(s);
    delete [] prev_string;
    return *this;
}

SimpleString&
SimpleString::operator=(const SimpleString& s)
{
    if( this == &s )
        return *this;
    return operator=(s._string);
}
```

Summary

Consistency is important in creating a class. Consistency must be achieved in both the external interface and the internal implementation of the class.

Externally, objects must behave consistently when manipulated by clients through the public interface of the class. A client deals with an object in terms of its logical state. A simple logical model is easier to understand, and consistent behavior promotes simplicity. Class `string` is hard to use because one of its operations always dynamically allocates sufficient memory, while another operation assumes that the client will only attempt to store a string that fits in the current array.

Internally, the implementation of a class must be self-consistent with respect to object state. Class invariant relationships between data members are one form of consistency. Consistent policies governing the management of dynamic memory are another form. Generally, the internal physical state model is more complicated than the logical model. The additional internal complexity is all the more reason to strive for consistency. Confusion in an object's implementation leads, at best, to inconsistent behavior, and more likely, to outright errors in behavior.

Bibliographic Notes

Object state is treated at length in Rumbaugh [3]. C++ has no language support for class invariants, but see Meyer [2] for a description of class invariants in Eiffel.

1. Kernighan, B. W., and Plauger, P. J. 1974 (2d ed., 1978). *The Elements of Programming Style.* New York, NY: McGraw-Hill.

2. Meyer, B. 1988. *Object-Oriented Software Construction.* Englewood Cliffs, NJ: Prentice-Hall.

3. Rumbaugh, J., Blaha, M., Premerlani, W., Eddy, F., and Lorensen, W. 1991. *Object-Oriented Modelling and Design.* Englewood Cliffs, NJ: Prentice-Hall.

Exercises

2.1. Which in-line functions in the code presented in this chapter are of doubtful value?

2.2. Examine class `string` in Listing 2.5. This string class uses reference counting so that different string objects with the same value sometimes share a common representation. Note the way `operator=(const string &)` works when a string object is assigned to itself. Which, if any, of the problems seen in the other string classes appear in this class?

Listing 2.5 Another class `string`

```
#include <iostream.h>
#include <string.h>
#include <stdlib.h>

class string {
    struct srep {
        char* s;         // pointer to data
        int   n;         // reference count
        srep() { n = 1; }
    };
    srep *p;
public:
    string(const char *);      // string x = "abc"
    string();                  // string x;
    string(const string &);    // string x = string ...
    string& operator=(const char *);
    string& operator=(const string &);
    ~string();
    char& operator[](int i);

    friend ostream& operator<<(ostream&, const string&);
    friend istream& operator>>(istream&, string&);

    friend int operator==(const string &x, const char *s)
        { return strcmp(x.p->s, s) == 0; }
```

```
      friend int operator==(const string &x, const string &y)
          { return strcmp(x.p->s, y.p->s) == 0; }

      friend int operator!=(const string &x, const char *s)
          { return strcmp(x.p->s, s) != 0; }

      friend int operator!=(const string &x, const string &y)
          { return strcmp(x.p->s, y.p->s) != 0; }
};

string::string()
{
    p = new srep;
    p->s = 0;
}

string::string(const string& x)
{
    x.p->n++;
    p = x.p;
}

string::string(const char* s)
{
    p = new srep;
    p->s = new char[ strlen(s)+1 ];
    strcpy(p->s, s);
}

string::~string()
{
    if (--p->n == 0 ) {
        delete[] p->s;
        delete p;
    }
}

string& string::operator=(const char* s)
{
    if (p->n > 1 ){          // disconnect self
        p->n--;
        p = new srep;
    }
    else                     // free old string
        delete[] p->s;

    p->s = new char[ strlen(s)+1 ];
    strcpy(p->s, s);
    return *this;
}
```

```
string& string::operator=(const string& x)
{
    x.p->n++; // protect against ``st = st''
    if (--p->n == 0 ) {
        delete[] p->s;
        delete p;
    }
    p = x.p;
    return *this;
}

ostream& operator<<(ostream& s, const string& x)
{
    return s << x.p->s << "\n";
}

istream& operator>>(istream& s, string& x)
{
    char buf[256];
    s >> buf;    // unsafe, might overflow
    x = buf;
    return s;
}

char & string::operator[](int i)
{
    if (i<0 || strlen(p->s)<i) abort();
    return p->s[i];
}

// sample driver:
// read and echo words from input
// at "done", output words in reverse order

int main()
{
    string x[100];
    int n;

    cout << "here we go\n";
    for (n = 0; cin>>x[n]; n++) {
        if (n==100)
            abort();
        string y;
        cout << (y = x[n]);
        if (y=="done") break;
    }
    cout << "here we go back again\n";
    for (int i=n-1; i>=0; i--) cout << x[i];
    return 0;
}
```

3

Unnecessary Inheritance

Although Chapter 2 carefully distinguished the interface of a class from its implementation, it was not done in the context of inheritance. To understand the inheritance relationship between a derived class and its base class, it is important to understand the interface and implementation parts of the relationship separately. This chapter examines a case that appears superficially to be a natural candidate for inheritance. However, closer study of the interface and implementation of the base and derived classes results in substantial changes to the code.

Style Example: Stacks

Listing 3.1 shows a program that defines classes CharStack, for stack-of-characters, and IntStack, for stack-of-integers. Examine and evaluate the classes. Are the abstractions sound? Do the interfaces work? Is the inheritance appropriate?

Some readers' immediate reaction to CharStack and IntStack may be that these classes should be written using parameterized types (templates) as proposed for ANSI C++ (see Ellis and Stroustrup, page 341). We ignore this alternative and concentrate on the program as written, for two reasons. First, it is important to understand, by applying the core of C++, how the structure of this program arose before we consider how it might be rewritten using an extension. The misunderstanding that led to this program could easily arise in situations for which parameterized types would not offer an alternative. Second, at the time of writing this book, implementations of parameterized types were not widely available; they may not be properly incorporated into C++ for some time. It would be premature to discuss style issues with respect to parameterized types before sufficient programming experience had accumulated to serve as guidance on how to use the feature well. A version of the code that has been rewritten using templates is shown at the end of the chapter.

Listing 3.1 Original `Stack`, `CharStack` and `IntStack`

```cpp
#include <assert.h>
#include <string.h>

class Stack {
    int     top;
    int     size;
protected:
    void    **vec;
public:
            Stack(int sz);
            ~Stack();
    void    *push();
    void    *pop();
};

Stack::Stack(int sz)
{
    vec = new void*[size = sz];
    top = 0;
}

Stack::~Stack()
{
    delete [] vec;
}

void *Stack::push()
{
    assert(top < size);
    return vec[top++];
}

void *Stack::pop()
{
    assert(top > 0);
    return vec[--top];
}

const int defaultStack = 128;
```

```
class CharStack : public Stack {
    char    *data;
public:
            CharStack();
            CharStack(int size);
            CharStack(int size, char *init);
            ~CharStack();
    void    push(char);
    char    pop();
};

CharStack::CharStack()  :  Stack(defaultStack)
{
    data = new char[defaultStack];
    for( int i = 0; i < defaultStack; ++i )
        vec[i] = &data[i];
}

CharStack::CharStack(int size)  :  Stack(size)
{
    data = new char[size];
    for( int i = 0; i < size; ++i )
        vec[i] = &data[i];
}

CharStack::CharStack(int size, char *init)  :  Stack(size)
{
    data = new char[size];
    for( int i = 0; i < size; ++i )
        vec[i] = &data[i];
    for( i = 0; i < strlen(init); ++i )
        *((char*)Stack::push()) = init[i];
}

CharStack::~CharStack()
{
    delete [] data;
}

void CharStack::push(char d)
{
    *((char*)Stack::push()) = d;
}

char CharStack::pop()
{
    return *((char*)Stack::pop());
}
```

```
class IntStack : public Stack {
    int    *data;
public:
           IntStack();
           IntStack(int size);
           ~IntStack();
    void   push(int);
    int    pop();
};

IntStack::IntStack() : Stack(defaultStack)
{
    data = new int[defaultStack];
    for( int i = 0; i < defaultStack; ++i )
        vec[i] = &data[i];
}

IntStack::IntStack(int size) : Stack(size)
{
    data = new int[size];
    for( int i = 0; i < size; ++i )
        vec[i] = &data[i];
}

IntStack::~IntStack()
{
    delete [] data;
}

void IntStack::push(int d)
{
    *((int*)Stack::push()) = d;
}

int IntStack::pop()
{
    return *((int*)Stack::pop());
}
```

The core of the design is that both CharStack and IntStack are stacks, thus having a common base class, Stack. The inheritance hierarchy is shown in Figure 3.1.

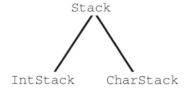

Figure 3.1 Inheritance hierarchy

We must look more closely at the program to discover that this inheritance is unnecessary and misleading and should be eliminated. Indeed, using public inheritance in this code creates a dangerous hole in the encapsulation of the stacks.

Inheritance Scope Rules

The public interface of the base class, `Stack`, is

```
public:
            Stack(int sz);
            ~Stack();
    void    *push();
    void    *pop();
};
```

Looking at the derived classes, we see member functions with the same names (`pop` and `push`) as those of the base class. Note that `Stack::pop()` and `Stack::push()` are not virtual functions. Also note that the types of the arguments in the derived member functions do not match the argument types for the corresponding base member function. For example, `Stack::push()` takes no arguments, while `IntStack::push()` takes an integer. For such functions, the scope rules of C++ mean that the members of the derived classes hide the base members, because a derived class introduces a new level of scope. The effect of the scope rules can be seen in the following example:

```
class Base {
public:
    void    f(float);
    void    g(float);
};

class Derived : public Base {
public:
    void    f(int);
};
```

```
int main()
{
    Derived d;

    d.f(1.5); // calls Derived::f
    d.g(1.5); // calls Base::g
```

The member functions named f are *not* overloaded. The derived class defines a function named f; therefore, the expression d.f(1.5) must call a derived member function named f. The expression d.g(1.5) calls the base member function because there is no derived member named g. In the search for g, the derived class is searched first; no member is found, so the base class is then searched. From a Derived object, Base::g can be reached by the name g, but Base::f cannot be reached by the name f.

The public interface of IntStack is

```
public:
            IntStack();
            IntStack(int size);
            ~IntStack();
    void    push(int);
    int     pop();
};
```

Under the scope rules outlined above, an IntStack or CharStack object is manipulated through its own push() and pop() member functions, not through the functions inherited from Stack. IntStack and CharStack inherit the public interface from Stack, but hide it behind their own functions. We will return to this matter later in the chapter.

Inheritance Relationships

For now, let's look at the inheritance relationships. Stack provides each of its derived classes with an indexing service over a protected vector, vec, of pointers-to-void. Stack adjusts a private integer member, top, to traverse the array in response to push and pop operations from the derived class. The derived class allocates its own vector, pointed to by data, for the values stored in the stack and initializes vec, so that for all i (within bounds), vec[i] points to data[i]. The pointers-to-void returned by Stack::push() and Stack::pop() tell the derived class on which element of data to operate for push and pop operations, respectively.

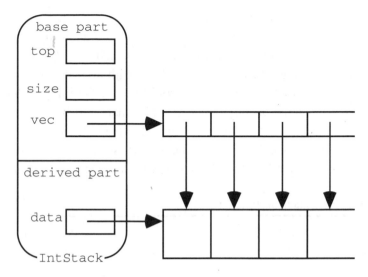

Figure 3.2 Pointers from vec to data array

The data structure is as shown in Figure 3.2. Notice the uniformity in the pattern of the pointers. The data structure contains little information. The derived class constructors execute

```
vec[i] = &data[i];
```

for each element of the array pointed to by data, to set the pointers in vec. After construction the pointers never change. The base class passes back these pointers to tell the derived class where to access data. Something is wrong; there are too many pointers for the small amount of information involved.

If we focus on the cast in IntStack::pop(), we see the situation from a different perspective.

```
int IntStack::pop()
{
    return *((int*)Stack::pop());
}
```

The cast converts the pointer-to-void returned by Stack::pop() to a pointer-to-int in order to access an element of the array pointed to by IntStack::data. To avoid the dangers inherent in casting, it is generally better to program without casts. This cast can be removed easily. Doing so will reveal the problem with vec. In general, `Stack::pop()` returns `vec[i]`, `vec[i]` points to `data[i]`, and `IntStack::pop()` returns `data[i]`. No cast would be needed if `Stack::pop()` delivered the index i directly, instead of `vec[i]`. Given i, `IntStack::pop()` immediately has `data[i]`, with no need to cast. The `push()` and `pop()` member functions of `Stack` could return the integer that the derived object really needs, instead of the pointer-to-`void` that must be cast before use. This simpler version of `Stack` is shown in Listing 3.2. Note that the `push()` and `pop()` members of `IntStack` and `CharStack` no longer use casts. Also note that the name of `Stack` has been changed to `StackIndex`, which better describes its abstraction.

Listing 3.2 Simplified stack abstraction

```
#include <assert.h>
#include <string.h>

class StackIndex {
    int     top;
    int     size;
public:
            StackIndex(int sz);
            ~StackIndex();
    int     push();
    int     pop();
};

StackIndex::StackIndex(int sz)
{
    size = sz;
    top = 0;
}

StackIndex::~StackIndex()
{
}

int StackIndex::push()
{
    assert(top < size);
    return top++;
}

int StackIndex::pop()
{
    assert(top > 0);
    return --top;
}
```

```
const int defaultStack = 128;

class CharStack : public StackIndex {
    char    *data;
public:
            CharStack();
            CharStack(int size);
            CharStack(int size, char *init);
            ~CharStack();
    void    push(char);
    char    pop();
};

CharStack::CharStack() : StackIndex(defaultStack)
{
    data = new char[defaultStack];
}

CharStack::CharStack(int size) : StackIndex(size)
{
    data = new char[size];
}

CharStack::CharStack(int size, char *init) : StackIndex(size)
{
    data = new char[size];
    for( int i = 0; i < strlen(init); ++i)
        data[StackIndex::push()] = init[i];
}

CharStack::~CharStack()
{
    delete [] data;
}

void CharStack::push(char d)
{
    data[StackIndex::push()] = d;
}

char CharStack::pop()
{
    return data[StackIndex::pop()];
}
```

```
class IntStack : public StackIndex {
    int     *data;
public:
            IntStack();
            IntStack(int size);
            ~IntStack();
    void    push(int);
    int     pop();
};

IntStack::IntStack() : StackIndex(defaultStack)
{
    data = new int[defaultStack];
}

IntStack::IntStack(int size) : StackIndex(size)
{
    data = new int[size];
}

IntStack::~IntStack()
{
    delete [] data;
}

void IntStack::push(int d)
{
    data[StackIndex::push()] = d;
}

int IntStack::pop()
{
    return data[StackIndex::pop()];
}
```

The new interface to class `StackIndex` better reflects the abstraction that it provides. The common abstraction is a moving index that tells the derived class where to access data. The information about how a stack behaves is confined to class `Stack`. The information about the elements in a particular stack is confined to the derived class. The only communication is in terms of integer indices. With no loss of function, the stack abstraction is made simpler. Its responsibilities are limited to maintaining an index so that another class can provide a stack.

▶ **Look for simple abstractions.**

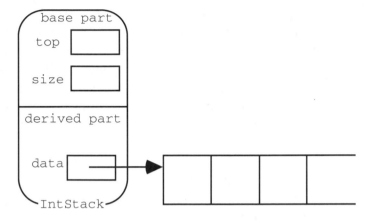

Figure 3.3 Simplified data structure

`Stack::vec` is redundant and has disappeared from class `StackIndex`. Each derived class obtains all the information it needs from the index returned by `StackIndex::push()` or `StackIndex::pop()`. There is no longer a reason for the base class to store pointers to the data declared in the derived classes. The data structure is now as shown in Figure 3.3. Making the program simpler has also made it more memory-efficient. The elimination of `Stack::vec` dramatically reduces the memory required for implementing a stack. On a typical 32-bit architecture, with 4-byte integers and 4-byte pointers, an `IntStack` object now uses only half the heap space compared with the original version: 4 bytes per element instead of 8. The heap space used by a `CharStack` object is reduced by a factor of 5, from 5 bytes per element to just 1.

Encapsulation

The new stack abstraction is simpler, and the program is smaller and uses less memory. Still, there is more to uncover about the inheritance relationships between `StackIndex` and its derived classes. We noted earlier in the chapter that the `push()` and `pop()` members of the derived classes hide their namesakes from the base class. However, using their fully resolved names, `StackIndex::push()` and `StackIndex::pop()` can be invoked on an `IntStack` or `CharStack` object. In fact, `StackIndex::push()` and `StackIndex::pop()` are called in this way from within their respective derived member functions.

The base `push()` and `pop()` member functions can even be invoked without resorting to the scope resolution operator. If an `IntStack` or `CharStack` object is accessed through a pointer-to-`StackIndex` or reference-to-`StackIndex`, then the name `pop` or `push` invokes the base member function. The accessibility of the base member functions is a serious breach of the encapsulation of stacks: It is possible for other parts of the program to drive a stack into an inconsistent state. The following function shows three ways to breach the encapsulation of `IntStack`:

```
void Violate()
{
    IntStack s;
    s.StackIndex::push();     // public member of public base
    StackIndex *p = &s;
    p->push();                // calls StackIndex::push
    StackIndex &r = s;
    r.push();                 // calls StackIndex::push
}
```

By calling the public base member directly, the `Violate` function advances the stack index without supplying a value to push on the stack. The effect is that the stack grows by one element, but since no value is supplied when the push is performed, the value returned later by `IntStack::pop()` is undefined. The popped value will be whatever value the array element's memory had at the time of the push.

We see that a client can directly manipulate the implementation of a stack, resulting in a stack object whose state is undefined. The encapsulation of the stack abstraction is flawed. The problem did not arise in modifying the code to eliminate the array of pointers in the base class. The hole in the encapsulation was present in the original code. The hole must be closed.

There is a second problem related to inheritance: The base destructor is not declared virtual. If an `IntStack` is created dynamically and later deleted through a pointer-to-base, only the base destructor will be called. In this respect, destructors behave like other member functions: The destructor is determined by the type of pointer.

```
IntStack *p = new IntStack;
// ...
StackIndex *q = p;
// ...
delete q; // calls only StackIndex::~StackIndex
```

Because the derived destructor may not be called, programs using classes `IntStack` or `CharStack` potentially have memory leaks. The memory leak in class `String` in Chapter 2 was the result of a missing `delete` in a member function. This memory leak arises even though the derived destructor is correct. The `delete` in the derived destructor can only execute if that destructor is called, which it will not be if a derived object is deleted through a base pointer. If the vector allocated for the stack's data is not deleted, the program will accumulate garbage and eventually run out of heap memory. Memory leaks are difficult to detect early in the software life cycle; small tests may not consume enough memory to produce noticeable symptoms. Chapter 7 shows how to instrument a program to monitor the use of heap memory and discover leaks.

The potential memory leak could be corrected by declaring a virtual destructor in the base class, but that would constitute a shortsighted patch that fails to address the real structural problems in the code. For these classes, we can find better solutions to this problem. We will return to the question of virtual base destructors in Chapters 4 and 9.

Indeed, there are two remedies, either of which solves both the encapsulation hole and the memory leak. The first remedy is to make `StackIndex` a private base class. Private inheritance inhibits the propagation of the public base interface to the public interface of the derived class and also prevents a pointer-to-base or reference-to-base from referring to a derived object. If `StackIndex` becomes a private base class, the `Violate` function generates a series of compile-time error messages:

```
class CharStack : private StackIndex {
// ...

class IntStack : private StackIndex {
// ...

void Violate()
{
    IntStack s;
    s.StackIndex::push();    // error
    StackIndex *p = &s;      // error
    p->push();
    StackIndex &r = s;       // error
    r.push();
}
```

The attempt to access the private base member is illegal, as are the attempts to make a pointer-to-private-base and a reference-to-private-base refer to a derived object. The destructor problem is also corrected. Since a pointer-to-private-base may not point to a derived object, the effect of a `delete` on such a pointer is moot.

Interface versus Implementation

Why use inheritance at all? If we examine the inheritance relationship more closely, we see that the inheritance can be eliminated entirely. The second remedy is to use a member object instead of inheritance.

As discussed in Chapter 2, a C++ class has two major elements: a public interface, which characterizes behavior, and a private implementation of that behavior. Most inheritance is from a public base class: The derived class inherits both interface and implementation. More selective inheritance, in which the derived class inherits either the interface or the implementation exclusively, is possible. From a private base class, a derived class inherits all of the implementation, but none of the interface. From a public abstract base class, the derived class inherits all of the interface, but the inherited implementation may be incomplete or nonexistent.

Every use of inheritance should be evaluated carefully. Is the inheritance for interface, implementation or both? In this program, `CharStack` and `IntStack` inherit only for implementation. The `CharStack` interface is similar to, but distinct from, the `IntStack` interface. Their member functions have the same names, but one deals in `char` values and the other in `int` values. `IntStack` and `CharStack` have no common interface; clients cannot treat their objects uniformly nor interchangeably. While the `IntStack` and `CharStack` abstractions are specializations of a stack abstraction, they are not specializations of the abstraction provided by `StackIndex`. An `IntStack` is *not* a kind of `StackIndex`. From the point of view of a client object, `StackIndex`, `IntStack` and `CharStack` all provide distinct services. `StackIndex` manages an index; `IntStack` manages a stack of integer values; and `CharStack` manages a stack of characters. The "is a kind of" relationship does not make sense from a client's perspective, and public inheritance is therefore inappropriate.

The relationship between a derived class and its private base class is similar to that between a client class and a server class. With `StackIndex` as a private base, `IntStack` and `CharStack` inherit from `StackIndex` in order to take advantage of `StackIndex`'s index management service. The derived classes are clients of `StackIndex`. An alternative way to express this relationship, without inheritance, is to embed a private member instance of `StackIndex` in each `IntStack` and `CharStack` object.

Instead of being a base class, StackIndex can be a private member object within CharStack and IntStack. This changes the structure of the program very little, as shown in Listing 3.3. The same service is provided by the same type of object. The difference is that the server is now a member object, not a private base, so the server is identified by a member name instead of a class name. In this case, the choice of private base class versus private member object is very much a matter of taste — the two constructions are functionally equivalent. For simplicity, however, a member object is preferable because the semantics of member objects are trivial compared to those of inheritance.

▶ **Recognize inheritance for implementation; use a private base class or (preferably) a member object.**

Listing 3.3 Member object replaces inheritance

```
#include <assert.h>
#include <string.h>

class StackIndex {
    int      top;
    int      size;
public:
             StackIndex(int sz);
    int      push();
    int      pop();
};

StackIndex::StackIndex(int sz)
{
    size = sz;
    top = 0;
}

int StackIndex::push()
{
    assert(top < size);
    return top++;
}

int StackIndex::pop()
{
    assert(top > 0);
    return --top;
}

const int defaultStack = 128;
```

```
class CharStack {
    StackIndex  index;
    char        *data;
public:
                CharStack();
                CharStack(int size);
                CharStack(int size, char *init);
                ~CharStack();
    void        push(char);
    char        pop();
};

CharStack::CharStack() : index(defaultStack)
{
    data = new char[defaultStack];
}

CharStack::CharStack(int size) : index(size)
{
    data = new char[size];
}

CharStack::CharStack(int size, char *init) : index(size)
{
    data = new char[size];
    for( int i = 0; i < strlen(init); ++i)
        data[index.push()] = init[i];
}

CharStack::~CharStack()
{
    delete [] data;
}

void CharStack::push(char d)
{
    data[index.push()] = d;
}

char CharStack::pop()
{
    return data[index.pop()];
}
```

```
class IntStack {
    StackIndex  index;
    int         *data;
public:
                IntStack();
                IntStack(int size);
                ~IntStack();
    void        push(int);
    int         pop();
};

IntStack::IntStack() : index(defaultStack)
{
    data = new int[defaultStack];
}

IntStack::IntStack(int size) : index(size)
{
    data = new int[size];
}

IntStack::~IntStack()
{
    delete [] data;
}

void IntStack::push(int d)
{
    data[index.push()] = d;
}

int IntStack::pop()
{
    return data[index.pop()];
}
```

Overloading versus Default Arguments

Before leaving this example, notice the similarities among the overloaded constructors of both `CharStack` and `IntStack`. As with the overloaded constructors for
class `string` in Chapter 2, default arguments should replace function overloading, as
shown for `CharStack` in Listing 3.4. For each class, multiple constructors collapse
into one, simplifying maintenance of the code. Conversion from function overloading
to default arguments is not always this straightforward, but should always be considered. Recall this guideline:

> ► **Consider default arguments as an alternative to function**
> **overloading.**

Finally, note that `CharStack::CharStack` in Listing 3.4 still calls `strlen()` on each iteration of its loop. If this constructor proves to be a performance bottleneck, it should be easy to fix.

Listing 3.4 Default arguments replace function overloading

```
class CharStack {
    StackIndex   index;
    char         *data;
public:
                 CharStack(int size = defaultStack, char *init = "");
                 ~CharStack();
    void         push(char);
    char         pop();
};

CharStack::CharStack(int size, char *init) : index(size)
{
    data = new char[size];
    for( int i = 0; i < strlen(init); ++i)
        data[index.push()] = init[i];
}
```

Templates

The common properties of `IntStack` and `CharStack` can be expressed quite differently using the new C++ mechanism of templates, also known as parameterized types. A class template for a stack class is shown in Listing 3.5.

Listing 3.5 `Stack` as a class template

```
const int defaultStack = 128;

template <class T>
class Stack {
    int      size;
    int      top;
    T        *data;
public:
             Stack(int size = defaultStack);
             ~Stack();
    void     push(T);
    T        pop();
};
```

```
template <class T>
Stack<T>::Stack(int s)
{
    size = s;
    top = 0;
    data = new T[size];
}

template <class T>
Stack<T>::~Stack()
{
    delete [] data;
}

template <class T>
void Stack<T>::push(T d)
{
    assert(top<size);
    data[top++] = d;
}

template <class T>
T Stack<T>::pop()
{
    assert(top>0);
    return data[--top];
}
```

The `Stack` class template defines a family of classes. When the `Stack` template is used to declare an object, a type must be supplied to occupy the place of the dummy type, `T`, in the template declaration. For example,

```
Stack<char> stackOfChar(10);
```

declares an object called `stackOfChar`, which is a stack that stores up to 10 `char` values, while

```
Stack<int> stackOfInt(20);
```

declares an object called `stackOfInt`, which is a stack that stores up to 20 `int` values. The type of the argument to `push()` and the return value from `pop()` are also the dummy type, `T`.

The principal motivation for the addition of templates to C++ is their support for general-purpose collection classes. Not only can stacks of integers and characters be created, but stacks of floating point numbers, stacks of pointers-to-`char`, etc., can be created as well.

The behavior of the objects instantiated from the class template differs in one subtle way from the behavior of those instantiated from the original declarations of `IntStack` and `CharStack`. The original `CharStack` constructor could take a second argument, which would specify a string of characters to push on the stack. But no `IntStack` constructor took such an argument. When using a template to describe both classes at once, there is no way to express such variation.

Summary

The first and most important change we made in this program was to the abstraction defined by class `Stack`. Originally, the interface was defined in terms of pointers into the client's array. The stack abstraction was simplified by expressing the interface in terms of an integer index. The resulting class, renamed `StackIndex`, more concisely captures the general properties of a stack, and ignores inessential representation detail. In general, the simpler an abstraction the better — as long as it remains sufficient. For this program, the simpler abstraction was safer, because several casts were eliminated, and more efficient, because an array of pointers was eliminated.

The second major change in the program corrected an encapsulation hole that was created by the use of public inheritance when the derived class needed only implementation from the base class. A private `StackIndex` member object was a simpler way for `CharStack` and `IntStack` to obtain the services of `StackIndex`.

Bibliographic Notes

The client–server model is described in Gorlen *et al.* [2] and Wirfs-Brock *et al.* [3]. The term "client" is also used to refer to the programmer of client code; the term "supplier" is sometimes used instead of server.

1.   Ellis, M. A., and Stroustrup, B. 1990. *The Annotated C++ Reference Manual.* Reading, MA: Addison-Wesley.

2. Gorlen, K. E., Orlow, S. M., and Plexico, P. S. 1990. *Data Abstraction and Object-Oriented Programming in C++*. Chichester, England: Wiley.

3. Wirfs-Block, R., Wilkerson, B., and Wiener, L. 1990. *Designing Object-Oriented Software*. Englewood Cliffs, NJ: Prentice-Hall.

Exercise

3.1. StackIndex can be either a private base class or a private member object of IntStack and CharStack. Construct situations in which there would not be such a choice. First, create a class that obtains the services of another class that *must* be incorporated as a private base class. Second, create a class in which a service *must* be incorporated as a private member object.

4

Virtual Functions

In Chapter 3 we made an important distinction between inheritance for interface and inheritance for implementation. The inheritance relationships studied in this chapter are clearly for interface — a natural "is a kind of" relationship is modelled, and public inheritance is appropriate. However, the decision to use public inheritance raises other questions with respect to the detailed distribution of the data and function members of the classes in the inheritance hierarchy. Which members should be protected? Which functions should be virtual? This chapter examines such topics.

Style Example: Vehicles and Garages

Listing 4.1 shows a program that manipulates vehicles, recording their entry and exit from a parking garage. Classes Car and Truck are derived from a common base class, Vehicle. The inheritance hierarchy is shown in Figure 4.1. Vehicles identify themselves by printing a message with the vehicle's type (car or truck) and license plate number.

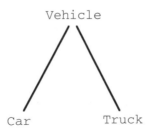

Figure 4.1 The Vehicle inheritance hierarchy

Listing 4.1 Vehicles and garages

```c
#include <stdio.h>
#include <string.h>

class Vehicle {
protected:
    char    *plate;
public:
            Vehicle() { plate = NULL; }
            Vehicle(char *p)
            {
                plate = new char[strlen(p)+1];
                strcpy(plate, p);
            }
            ~Vehicle() { delete [] plate; }
virtual
    void    identify()
            {
                printf("generic vehicle\n");
            }
};

class Car : public Vehicle {
public:
            Car() : Vehicle() { }
            Car(char *p) : Vehicle(p) { }
    void    identify()
            {
                printf("car with plate %s\n", plate);
            }
};

class Truck : public Vehicle {
public:
            Truck() : Vehicle() { }
            Truck(char *p) : Vehicle(p) { }
    void    identify()
            {
                printf("truck with plate %s\n", plate);
            }
};
```

```
class Garage {
    int     maxVehicles;
    Vehicle **parked;
public:
            Garage(int max);
            ~Garage();
    int     accept(Vehicle*);
    Vehicle *release(int bay);
    void    listVehicles();
};

Garage::Garage(int max)
{
    maxVehicles = max;
    parked = new Vehicle*[maxVehicles];
    for( int bay = 0; bay < maxVehicles; ++bay )
        parked[bay] = NULL;
}

Garage::~Garage()
{
    delete [] parked;
}

int Garage::accept(Vehicle *veh)
{
    for( int bay = 0; bay < maxVehicles; ++bay )
        if( !parked[bay] ) {
            parked[bay] = veh;
            return bay;
        }
    return -1;      // no bay available
}

Vehicle *Garage::release(int bay)
{
    if( bay < 0 || bay >= maxVehicles )
        return NULL;
    Vehicle *veh = parked[bay];
    parked[bay] = NULL;
    return veh;
}

void Garage::listVehicles()
{
    for( int bay = 0; bay < maxVehicles; ++bay )
        if( parked[bay] ){
            printf("Vehicle in bay %d is: ", bay);
            parked[bay]->identify();
        }
}
```

```
Car c1("RVR 101");
Car c2("SPT 202");
Car c3("CHP 303");
Car c4("BDY 404");
Car c5("BCH 505");

Truck t1("TBL 606");
Truck t2("IKY 707");
Truck t3("FFY 808");
Truck t4("PCS 909");
Truck t5("SLY 000");

int main()
{
    Garage Park(15);

    Park.accept(&c1);

    int t2bay = Park.accept(&t2);

    Park.accept(&c3);
    Park.accept(&t1);

    int c4bay = Park.accept(&c4);

    Park.accept(&c5);
    Park.accept(&t5);

    Park.release(t2bay);

    Park.accept(&t4);
    Park.accept(&t3);

    Park.release(c4bay);

    Park.accept(&c2);

    Park.listVehicles();

    return 0;
}
```

The output from the program in Listing 4.1 is

```
Vehicle in bay 0 is: car with plate RVR 101
Vehicle in bay 1 is: truck with plate PCS 909
Vehicle in bay 2 is: car with plate CHP 303
Vehicle in bay 3 is: truck with plate TBL 606
Vehicle in bay 4 is: car with plate SPT 202
Vehicle in bay 5 is: car with plate BCH 505
Vehicle in bay 6 is: truck with plate SLY 000
Vehicle in bay 7 is: truck with plate FFY 808
```

The `main()` function exercises the `Garage` class by inserting and removing `Truck` and `Car` objects from a `Garage` object called `Park`. The public interface to class `Garage` is defined in terms of pointers to `Vehicle` objects. `Garage::accept(Vehicle*)` finds an empty parking bay, if one exists, in which to place a vehicle. `Garage::release(int)` returns a pointer to the vehicle occupying a given bay and empties that bay. `Garage::ListVehicles()` lists, by bay number, all the vehicles in the garage. Note that `Garage` is more than just a bounded collection of pointers-to-`Vehicle`. Each vehicle registered in the garage has an associated bay number, the only key by which it may be referred to within the `Garage`. This access by key is seen most clearly in the interface to `release()`: A vehicle is removed from the garage by giving its bay number, not by a pointer to a `Vehicle` object.

Study Listing 4.1. How would you rewrite this program, and why? There is a subtle bug in the interaction between the base class and its derived classes. There are also many variations in the way the member functions of the classes might be rewritten. Think first about correctness, second about simplicity, and finally about execution time and memory consumption. (Assume that the performance of the linear search in `Garage::accept()` is satisfactory.)

Consistency

Chapter 2 discussed consistency in class design: The need for external consistency in the interface, and internal consistency in the implementation of each object's state. When inheritance is used, there is a further issue of consistency to consider: consistency in the interface between a base class and its derived classes. In addition to the public interface, a base class may have a *protected interface* consisting of the protected members accessible from derived classes. By declaring protected members, a base class provides special access for use by its derived classes. The derived classes must use this access consistently with the implementation of the base class.

Classes `Car` and `Truck` make inconsistent use of the base protected member `plate`. `Vehicle`, `Car` and `Truck` all have default constructors, that is, constructors that require no arguments. The initializer lists of the derived default constructors invoke the base default constructor. The base default constructor, `Vehicle::Vehicle()`, sets `plate` to the null pointer, indicating that there is no license plate number:

```
Vehicle() { plate = NULL; }
```

However, the `identify()` functions in both `Car` and `Truck` pass `plate` to `printf()` without checking for a null value. The `printf()` call in `Car::identify()` is

```
printf("car with plate %s\n", plate);
```

The `printf()` call in `Truck::identify()` is

```
printf("truck with plate %s\n", plate);
```

If `plate` is a null pointer, the behavior of `printf()` will be undefined. Given a null pointer for `%s` conversion, some implementations of `printf()` write an error message, others write garbage, and still others simply crash with an address fault. The following code, which instantiates a `Truck` object and calls its `identify()` member function, shows how easily the undefined situation can arise:

```
{
    Truck t;
    t.identify();
}
```

The root of the problem is in the `identify()` member functions of the derived classes. They behave inconsistently with respect to the protected interface of their base class. The base class represents a missing license plate number with a null pointer, but the derived `identify()` functions assume that the pointer is always non-null.

A derived class cannot be coded before its base class. A derived class is written at the same time as, or after, its base class and should conform consistently to the conventions established by the base class. The derived class is obliged to interact correctly with the protected members of its base class. In `Car::identify()` and `Truck::identify()`, the error is one of omission: The derived classes do not account for all of the legitimate states of the base part of their objects.

In the case of `Car` and `Truck`, the error is narrowly contained. The omission in the derived classes affects only the derived classes — only the derived member functions misbehave. A similar, but more serious, error would occur if a derived member function *modified* a base protected member inconsistently. A base protected member assigned an inconsistent value might cause a base member function, or a member function of another derived class, to fail. For example, if `Vehicle` were written under the assumption that `plate` is always non-null, but a member function of one derived class set the pointer to null, then any member function — base or derived, even from a different derived class — that assumes that plate is non-null might fail.

> ▶ **A derived class must treat inherited state consistently**
> **with its base class.**

To correct the bug, the derived `identify()` functions should test for a null pointer and take reasonable action to handle that case. Substituting another string for the null pointer is a benign approach. The substitution could be either an empty string or a string that indicates that the plate number is missing. The definition of `Car::identify()` could be written as

```
void    identify()
        {
            char *p = plate ? plate : "<none>";
            printf("car with plate %s\n", p);
        }
```

The correction for `Truck::identify()` is similar.

Base Destructors

Another important property of the interface between this base class and its derived classes is that `Vehicle` has a non-virtual destructor. The non-virtual base destructor in class `Stack` in Chapter 3 became a moot issue when the public inheritance was eliminated. For `Vehicle`, we again have a base class whose destructor is non-virtual. As the program stands, the non-virtual base destructor causes no problems, because the derived classes do not define destructors. As long as the derived classes do not need destructors, the base class may remain as it is.

> ▶ **If a public base class does not have a virtual destructor,**
> **no derived class nor members of a derived class should**
> **have a destructor.**

This rule does not adequately address multiple inheritance. See Chapter 9 for discussion of virtual base destructors under multiple inheritance.

If a derived class or a member of a derived class does define a destructor, and the base destructor remains non-virtual, memory leaks or other abnormalities can ensue. Suppose a static member is added to class Car to record the number of Car objects that are active at any time. The counter must be incremented by each Car constructor and decremented by a destructor:

```
class Car : public Vehicle {
    static int active;
public:
        Car() : Vehicle() { ++active; }
        Car(char *p) : Vehicle(p) { ++active; }
        ~Car() { --active; }
    // ...
};

int Car::active = 0;
```

Car has a destructor, but it will only be executed at the end of the lifetime of an object that is known at compile-time to be an instance of Car. When a dynamic object is deleted, its type may not be known at compile-time, since a pointer-to-base may point to a base or a derived object. Consider the following code, in which a Car object is deleted through a pointer-to-Vehicle:

```
Vehicle *p = new Car;

// ...

delete p;
```

As with other non-virtual member functions, the binding that determines which destructor is called from the delete expression is made at compile-time based on the type of the pointer in the expression. Because p is of type pointer-to-base and the base destructor is non-virtual, only the base destructor executes, and the Car::active counter is not decremented. The problem is corrected by making the base destructor virtual. Like other virtual functions, the binding for virtual destructors is determined at run-time by the class of the object pointed to in the delete expression.

One way to eliminate concern about whether the correct destructors are executing is to make all base destructors virtual. There is then no need to modify the base class in response to changes in derived classes. We will make the `Vehicle` destructor virtual, as shown below.

> ▶ **Usually, the destructor in a public base class should be virtual.**

Having corrected one bug in the interface between the base and derived classes and identified another potential one, we can now examine the inheritance relationship more closely.

Inheritance

The inheritance hierarchy in this program is sound. Both `Car` and `Truck` are specializations of the base class `Vehicle`. Class `Garage` manages cars and trucks uniformly with respect to the base class interface. The public inheritance establishes valid "is a kind of" relationships between the base and the derived classes: A `Truck` is a kind of `Vehicle`; a `Car` is a kind of `Vehicle`. Other parts of the program can deal with `Car` and `Truck` objects knowing only that they are at least `Vehicle` objects and that they react to the interface established by the public members of `Vehicle`.

Although the underlying inheritance is valid, the detailed distribution of code between the base and derived classes can be improved. As discussed in Chapter 1, a base class should characterize all the properties of the abstraction that are common to its objects and the objects of its derived classes. When common state and common behavior are captured in the base class, a single description serves many classes. If common properties are not identified and placed in the base class, they must be replicated in each derived class. The replication makes the program harder to write, read and maintain. When using public inheritance to construct "is a kind of" relationships, always ask two important questions:

- What is common among the classes of an inheritance hierarchy?
- What are the differences between the derived classes?

To be more succinct, what is the same, and what is different? Answering these questions provides valuable guidance on how to define an inheritance hierarchy of classes. The questions should be asked first about the public interfaces of the classes and then about their implementations. Many design issues are resolved by identifying commonality and differences among classes.

Thus, the first question in this case is what do the classes in the Vehicle hierarchy have in common? The common properties of all vehicles are a license plate number and the ability to identify themselves. These properties are captured appropriately in the base class as a data member, plate, and a virtual member function, identify(). The second question is what are the differences between Car and Truck? The only difference is the string "car" versus the string "truck" as the vehicle's textual description printed by the derived identify() functions. Car and Truck differ only in a value — a string — but not otherwise in their behavior.

The similarity between the definitions of Car::identify() and Truck::identify() is telling. Car::identify() is defined as

```
void    identify()
        {
            char *p = plate ? plate : "<none>";
            printf("car with plate %s\n", p);
        }
```

Truck::identify() is defined as

```
void    identify()
        {
            char *p = plate ? plate : "<none>";
            printf("truck with plate %s\n", p);
        }
```

Car and Truck have almost the same code in their respective versions of identify(). The base class does not fully describe the common properties of the derived classes. Their common printing behavior should become part of the base class. The code for the derived classes needs to differ only where the derived classes necessarily differ, that is, in the characteristic string, "car" or "truck". If the derived classes delivered just the string, the base class could undertake the remainder of the printing behavior.

The details of how to print should be moved to the base class. Vehicle::identify() will grow, but a single copy of the printing code in the base class will replace the copy in each derived class. The derived classes will shrink; their responsibility is reduced to that of providing an appropriate characteristic string.

▶ **Migrate common behavior to the base class.**

A new virtual function can be used to distinguish between derived objects. Adding a pure virtual function, group(), to Vehicle enables each derived class to override the function and deliver its characteristic string:

```
class Vehicle {
    char    *plate;
protected:
virtual
    char    *group() = 0;
public:
            Vehicle() { plate = NULL; }
            Vehicle(char *p)
            {
                plate = new char[strlen(p)+1];
                strcpy(plate, p);
            }
virtual     ~Vehicle() { delete [] plate; }
    void    identify()
            {
                char *p = plate ? plate : "<none>";
                printf("%s with plate %s\n", group(), p);
            }
};
```

Since group() accounts for the difference between the derived classes, there is no reason for identify() to be a virtual member function. The identify() function needs to be defined only in the base class. Essentially, the virtual behavior of identify() has been replaced with the virtual behavior of group(). We see below, in a transformation similar to one from Chapter 1, that group() itself may be replaced with a data member. Corresponding to this version of Vehicle, the Truck and Car classes become

```
class Car : public Vehicle {
    char    *group() { return "car"; }
public:
            Car() : Vehicle() {}
            Car(char *p) : Vehicle(p) { }
};

class Truck : public Vehicle {
    char    *group() { return "truck"; }
public:
            Truck() : Vehicle() {}
            Truck(char *p) : Vehicle(p) { }
};
```

Two other changes have been made to the program. First, `Vehicle::group()` is a pure virtual function, making `Vehicle` an abstract base class. The original `Vehicle` class had no meaningful implementation of `identify()`; the function's body was a dummy. It is better to denote formally, by making it an abstract base class, that `Vehicle` itself will not be instantiated. Programmers then know not to try to instantiate the class, and this is verified by the compiler. Second, the access level for `Vehicle::plate` has changed from protected to private. The printing behavior that depends on `plate` is now isolated in the base class. Restricting access to `plate` to the base class eliminates the opportunity to misuse it. Originally, the derived class interacted with two members of the base, `identify()` and `plate`, incorrectly in the case of `plate`. As modified, the derived class must still override a virtual function, but no longer has to interact with a data member. The interface between the base and derived classes is smaller.

Coupling

In the original program, the derived classes interacted in three ways with the base class. First, a derived constructor supplied an argument for a base constructor. Second, the derived classes had to define their own versions of `identify()`. Third, the derived `identify()` functions accessed the value of the `plate` member from the base. The revised versions of the classes interact in just two ways. The constructors are unchanged, but the single interaction through `group()` replaces the interactions that involved both `identify()` and `plate`.

Constantine originated use of the term *coupling* to describe the degree to which software components interact. In each interaction, one component exploits part of the interface supplied by another, and each kind of interaction increases the extent to which one component depends on the other. Coupling measures the amount of interaction and dependency between components. Though coupling could be formally defined as a numeric metric, we use the term informally and subjectively. The more one software component depends on another, the more *highly coupled* the components are said to be. Two components that do not interact at all are said to be *uncoupled*. In general, higher coupling between the components of a program makes the program harder to maintain, because there are more interactions to understand and preserve as the program is modified. Lower coupling, that is, fewer and simpler interactions, characterizes software that is easier to understand and maintain.

The introduction of group() has reduced the coupling between Vehicle and its derived classes. Instead of three interactions between the base and derived classes, there are now only two. The constructors still interact as before, but the two interactions involving identify() and plate have been replaced by a single, and equally simple, interaction involving group().

▶ **Reduce coupling — minimize interactions between classes.**

Value versus Behavior

Vehicle::identify() was a virtual function in the original version of the program, and following that style, group() is virtual in the revised version. Is a virtual function the right way to capture the difference between the characteristic strings "car" and "truck"? The difference between the derived classes is one of value, not one of behavior. Objects of the derived classes do not behave differently nor use different algorithms. A difference in value can be recorded more naturally in a data member than in a virtual function. A data member in Vehicle would be sufficient:

```
class Vehicle {
    char    *plate;
    char    *group;
public:
```

The data member can receive its value from an additional argument to each Vehicle constructor, supplied by the corresponding derived constructor. The base and derived classes then interact only during initialization, further reducing their coupling. Of the three kinds of interaction between the original classes, only constructor interaction remains. Versions of Vehicle, Truck and Car in this style are shown in Listing 4.2. A rule from Chapter 1 is applicable:

▶ **Use data members for variation in value; reserve virtual functions for variation in behavior.**

Listing 4.2 Data member replaces virtual function

```
class Vehicle {
    char    *plate;
    char    *group;
public:
            Vehicle(char *g)
            {
                group = g;
                plate = NULL;
            }
            Vehicle(char *g, char *p)
            {
                group = g;
                plate = new char[strlen(p)+1];
                strcpy(plate, p);
            }
virtual     ~Vehicle() { delete [] plate; }
    void    identify()
            {
                char *p = plate ? plate : "<none>";
                printf("%s with plate %s\n", group, plate);
            }
};

class Car : public Vehicle {
public:
            Car() : Vehicle("car") { }
            Car(char *p) : Vehicle("car", p) { }
};

class Truck : public Vehicle {
public:
            Truck() : Vehicle("truck") { }
            Truck(char *p) : Vehicle("truck", p) { }
};
```

Between the programs in Listings 4.1 and 4.2, class `Vehicle` has grown, while `Car` and `Truck` have diminished. This is the direct result of identifying common properties of the classes and moving them to the base class. Coding and maintenance are simplified if information is expressed once in the base class rather than repeated in each derived class.

Data versus Functions

The net change in class `Vehicle` is that the virtual `identify()` function has been replaced by a non-virtual `identify()` function and a private data member, `group`. In general, recording information in data is simpler than recording the same information in functions, and non-virtual functions are easier to understand than virtual functions.

When deciding whether to use a data member or a function member for a feature that must be included in a class, first ask:

- Is the feature characterized by a value or a behavior?

If the feature is a value, it is represented more simply as a data member. Objects of a derived class inherit the data member and may use the value. If the feature is a behavior — an action or an algorithm — then it should be implemented as a member function. Each member function is either virtual or non-virtual. So, for features characterized by the behavior of classes in an inheritance tree, there is a further question to ask:

- Do the derived classes have the same behavior as the base class?

If derived classes must exhibit different behaviors, then a virtual function must be used so that each derived class can provide its own implementation. If all the derived classes exhibit the same behavior, then they can share a common non-virtual member function defined by the base class.

In the early stages of writing a C++ program, it can be difficult to tell whether all the derived classes from a base will exhibit the same behavior for a given member function. A non-virtual member function may be adequate initially, but may have to be converted to a virtual function later because a derived class eventually appears that needs its own behavior. Is it better to plan for this by making the function virtual from the outset, or to wait until the need arises? If the virtual function is in place from the outset but never used, we pay the price of unnecessary flexibility. Since foresight is rarely perfect, most designs end up being either too narrow and specific or too broad and general. Given a choice of two mistakes, is it better to be too narrow or too broad? A narrow design may constrain the program later. But when the constraints become obvious, it is often easy to correct the program, for example, by making a base member function virtual. A design that is too broad will encounter problems sooner. When a design is broadened to handle more general cases, the difficulty is not knowing where to stop. If there are no constraints on the generalization process, a class can end up loaded with unnecessary code, making it harder to implement and use. It is harder to control an overgeneralized design than loosen a design that is too specific.

▶ **No class is perfect; too narrow a design is better than too broad.**

This rule assumes that the necessary classes are all under the programmer's control. Some C++ programmers do not have the luxury of going back to a base class to modify it on demand. A programmer who derives from a base class in a library supplied in binary, for which the only source is header files, cannot make arbitrary changes to resolve shortcomings in a base class. Programming with inheritance from such a library is much more difficult than in the case where the programmer controls all the source text. The creator of such a library must consider very carefully how the library may be extended by inheritance. Building a library that is shipped in binary and which other programmers are to extend by inheritance is extremely difficult, calling for exceptional understanding of the application domain and the C++ programming language. The skills needed to design and build such an extensible C++ library are beyond the scope of this book.

Object Size

Reduced coupling supports the decision that `group` should be a data member of `Vehicle`, rather than a virtual function. Thus, for programs in which simplicity is the main focus, `group` should be, without question, a data member. In other cases, the programmer must weigh simplicity against efficiency, in terms of object size and execution time. The tradeoffs of simplicity versus space and time can be quite subtle in C++. How much space and time does a data member take compared with the corresponding virtual function?

The space and time costs of simple data members are straightforward. Each data member of a class consumes space in each object of the class. As a data member of `Vehicle`, `group` makes each `Vehicle` object (and each derived object) larger by the size of a pointer-to-`char`. (We are not concerned here with static members, which consume no per-object space.) The cost in execution time to access a data member from within an expression in a function is apparent in the source code of the expression. The only detail to remember is the extra indirection involved in accessing a data member through the `this` pointer. For example, where `Vehicle::identify()` accesses `group`,

```
printf("%s with plate %s\n", group, plate);
```

`group` is equivalent to `this->group`. So, the space and time costs associated with using a data member are easily determined.

By comparison, the costs of virtual functions are harder to determine. In most implementations of C++, each object of a class that has at least one virtual function contains a special pointer, the "virtuals pointer," or "V-pointer." The V-pointer points to a table of virtual function descriptors, the "V-table" (see Ellis and Stroustrup, page 227). Only one V-pointer per object is needed, regardless of the number of virtual functions defined in the class. Moreover, all objects of the same class share a common V-table. Therefore, the size of an object grows by one pointer for the first virtual function in the class, but grows no more for additional virtual functions. The execution costs of virtual functions must also be considered. In typical implementations, a virtual function call is somewhat slower than a regular function call, because the calling expression must index the object's V-table to find the function to call. The additional work per call amounts to two or three instructions and two or three memory references. Whether or not this cost is significant in terms of overall performance depends on the frequency of calls to the function and the time taken to execute the function itself.

`Vehicle` objects already contain a V-pointer because their destructor is virtual. Therefore, adding `group()` as a virtual function of `Vehicle` does not increase the size of `Vehicle` objects. Adding `group` as a data member does increase the size of `Vehicle` objects, but eliminates a virtual function call from `identify()`. In summary, in deciding how to implement `group`, choose the virtual function to minimize object size and choose the data member for faster execution and simplicity.

Default Arguments

There is yet another tradeoff to face: default arguments versus function overloading. A similar situation arose in Chapter 2, though not involving inheritance. The same rule applies here:

> ▶ **Consider default arguments as an alternative to function**
> **overloading.**

The base and derived classes each have two constructors. The pairs of constructors differ in the second argument, which is treated as a null pointer in the constructor with just a single argument. Default arguments would remove half of the constructors, as shown in Listing 4.3. The number of constructors has been reduced, but at the expense of increasing the coupling between the base and derived classes. The decision governing the default license plate value has moved from the base to the derived class. Dependency between the classes has increased. Since `group` is no longer a virtual function, the `Vehicle` destructor is now a pure virtual function so that `Vehicle` remains an abstract base class.

Listing 4.3 Default arguments

```
class Vehicle {
    char    *plate;
    char    *group;
public:
            Vehicle(char *g, char *p);
virtual     ~Vehicle() = 0;
    void    identify();
};

Vehicle::Vehicle(char *g, char *p)
{
    group = g;
    if( p ) {
        plate = new char[strlen(p)+1];
        strcpy(plate, p);
    } else
        plate = NULL;
}

Vehicle::~Vehicle()
{
    delete [] plate;
}

void Vehicle::identify()
{
    char *p = plate ? plate : "<none>";
    printf("%s with plate %s\n", group, plate);
}

class Car : public Vehicle {
public:
            Car(char *p = NULL) : Vehicle("car", p) { }
};

class Truck : public Vehicle {
public:
            Truck(char *p = NULL) : Vehicle("truck", p) { }
};
```

Note that none of the `Vehicle` member functions is in-line in Listing 4.3. It is hard to believe that any of these members would need to be in-line functions for performance reasons, and some of them are becoming too large to fit comfortably in the class declaration. As mentioned in Chapter 0, member functions are often in-lined just to shorten a source program. Do not take seriously the in-line functions in Listings 4.1 and 4.2.

Summary

Compare the declarations of `Car` and `Truck` in Listing 4.3 with those in Listing 4.1. The derived classes are smaller in the final version because they now contain only the information about the differences between `Car` and `Truck` objects. The transformations have gradually moved common properties to the base class, leaving only the differences in the derived classes.

Bibliographic Notes

See Booch [1] or Budd [2] for a discussion of coupling in the context of object-oriented programming. For the origins of coupling in structured design, see Stevens *et al*. [4].

1. Booch, G. 1990. *Object-Oriented Design with Applications*. Redwood City, CA: Benjamin/Cummings.

2. Budd, T. 1991. *An Introduction to Object-Oriented Programming*. Reading, MA: Addison-Wesley.

3. Ellis, M. A., and Stroustrup, B. 1990. *The Annotated C++ Reference Manual*. Reading, MA: Addison-Wesley.

4. Stevens, W., Meyers, G., and Constantine, L. 1979. "Structured Design." In *Classics in Software Engineering*, Yourdon, E., ed. New York, NY: Yourdon Press.

Exercise

4.1. In Listing 4.3, `Vehicle::~Vehicle()` deletes `plate`, but not `group`. Why?

5

Operator Overloading

Operator overloading is deceptive. Simple examples demonstrate its notational convenience but understate the precise attention to detail demanded for its use in production programs. A programmer's good intentions are not enough to make operator overloading work effectively; the programmer must exercise great care to ensure that the benefits are achieved while the potential pitfalls are avoided. This chapter presents some generally accepted principles for good operator overloading and then demonstrates how difficult they can be to follow in practice.

Operator Overloading Basics

Most experts agree about the basic rules of successful operator overloading, and most programmers attempt to follow these rules. The first universally accepted tenet is that the overloading should not abuse the familiar language syntax. The built-in operators have established meanings and properties; overloading should not invalidate other programmers' expectations of how programs will behave.

The temptation to overload for cleverness can be irresistible. For example, in nontechnical language, the exclamation point is an attention grabber. Why not use the same symbol for issuing warning messages from a program? The ! operator could be overloaded for a string class in order to write a warning message to a console:

```
class String {
public:
        String(const char *);
// ...
        void operator! ();  // display warning
// ...
};

// ...

    String low_msg = "paper low";
    // ...
    if( level < THRESHOLD )
        !low_msg;
```

Such overloading only obscures. The amusement is temporary, but the burden of remembering what ! means and recognizing it accurately remains for the life of the software. For the sake of maintenance programmers, if you cannot resist the temptation to be clever, put such overloading in an unused prototype, not in production code.

Kernighan and Plauger's first rule of programming style is

▶ **Write clearly — don't be too clever.**

Their advice is to avoid exploiting covert properties of a programming language for the sake of a slick exhibition (p. 2). Operator overloading adds another dimension to programming, effectively giving the programmer the power to extend the programming language. Any power comes with the responsibility not to abuse it. Kernighan and Plauger caution against unwarranted cleverness in writing programs. With operator overloading we must also avoid such cleverness in the way the programming language is extended.

▶ **The meaning of an overloaded operator should be natural, not clever.**

This rule is by no means sufficient. An example of overloading with a natural interpretation is the use of ^ (the built-in exclusive OR operator) to mean exponentiation (a^b) over a numeric class, for which +, −, * and / have already been defined. Although the ^ itself is intuitively appropriate for the operation (it is the exponentiation operator in some languages), the choice does not serve well as an exponentiation operator in C++. Unfortunately, the difficulties are not apparent at first sight.

If ^ is overloaded for exponentiation, simple expressions do behave as expected. For example, b^c evaluates correctly. However, a slightly more complicated expression will not produce the intended result because of the precedence rules that govern all C++ operators:

```
b^c+d
```

Conventional notation dictates that exponentiation has higher precedence than addition — exponentiation is performed before addition, unless parentheses explicitly direct otherwise. Most programming languages with algebraic expressions that include exponentiation conform to this convention. (There are exceptions, such as APL, in which all operators have equal precedence.) Operator precedence in C++ is fixed, however, and ^ has lower precedence than +. If ^ is used for exponentiation, b^c+d must be written as

```
(b^c)+d
```

Choosing ^ for exponentiation places a burden on the programmers who write and read the code to remember that this operator has an unnatural precedence because it differs from established mathematical convention. Since the virtue of operator overloading is as notational convenience, an unnatural overloading defeats the purpose. An overloaded operator must be chosen not only for its lexical appeal, but also for its interaction with other operators.

> ▶ **An overloaded operator must interact appropriately with other operators.**

If the properties of an operator do match the semantics of the domain, there are other basic rules to follow. Consider + overloaded in a domain where addition is commutative, that is, x+y always equals y+x. There are two cases to consider. In the first case, if only one class, Point, is involved, then one operator function, such as

```
Point operator+(Point, Point);
```

is sufficient. The commutativity of + is achieved by a single operator function whose semantics do not depend on the order of its operands. In the second case, if a commutative operator is defined such that the left and right operands differ in type, the situation is more complex. Commutativity then demands that a set of operator functions be defined to take any combination of argument types. If, for example, the sum of a Point and a Rectangle is defined as

```
Rectangle operator+(Point, Rectangle);
```

then p+r can be written, but r+p cannot, where p is a `Point` and r is a `Rectangle`. The expression r+p causes a compile-time error because the operand types do not match (and, we assume, cannot be converted to) the operator function's argument types. The simplest way to make + commutative, and permit r+p, is to add another operator function:

```
Rectangle operator+(Rectangle, Point);
```

The implementation of this operator function is trivial, since all it does is transpose the arguments and call the original:

```
Rectangle operator+(Rectangle rect, Point pt)
{
    return pt+rect;
}
```

If defined as an in-line function, the argument-switching performed by this operator function will incur no run-time overhead.

The behavior of an overloaded operator should be consistent with any other algebraic rules of its domain and the behavior of other C++ operators. Another example of consistency is that > and < should be overloaded such that a>b and b<a are equivalent.

▶ **Overload operators consistently.**

Many operators are members of families of related operators, where overloading one member of a family makes it natural to overload others. If binary + is overloaded to mean addition, and unary – is overloaded to mean negation, then

```
    x + - y
```

may be written. This expression is exactly the definition of another member of this family: binary –. To make the family *complete*, binary – should be overloaded with semantics that are consistent with its conventional meaning, and unary + should be overloaded as well.

▶ **A set of overloaded operators should be complete.**

Finally, for the basic rules for operator overloading, recall from Chapter 2 the discussion of assignment for class `SimpleString` and the need to recognize the special case where the left-hand and right-hand sides of the assignment refer to the same object.

▶ **When defining `operator=`, remember x = x.**

There is a common thread to all these rules. Operator overloading capitalizes on a programmer's knowledge of algebra and the properties of C++ operators. Overloaded operators must behave in the way that a programmer with this knowledge would expect. If a programmer is surprised by anomalous behavior, or must work to remember a counterintuitive set of rules, the operator overloading is of dubious value. In summary,

▶ **When overloading operators, avoid surprises.**

We discover in the remainder of this chapter that surprises are hard to avoid.

Operator Overloading in Practice

Most programmers readily accept the general principles stated in the above rules. Unfortunately, applying the rules in practice is harder than expected. The overall goal of avoiding surprises calls for a detailed study of the many kinds of semantic interactions that occur in C++ programs. Before deciding to overload a set of operators, a programmer must consider which interactions with other language features may occur. The following list of features includes some that can interact adversely with operator overloading:

- implicit promotions and conversions
- programmer-defined conversions
- reference conversions
- pointer conversions
- `const` type qualifiers and their conversions
- overloading ambiguity resolution rules
- default arguments
- default assignment operators

- constructors

- temporary objects

- inheritance

Even if just a few of these features interact within a single expression, the semantics quickly become complicated, and the likelihood of a surprise effect rises dramatically. In this chapter we examine an example of operator overloading that is superficially natural, but hides subtle interactions.

Style Example: Class `FileArray`

Class `FileArray` in Listing 5.1 overloads `operator[]` to enable expressions of the form

```
file[index]
```

to read and write the individual bytes in a disk file. When the indexing operation appears on the left-hand side of an assignment expression, a character is written to the corresponding position in the file:

```
file[index] = value;
```

When the indexing is on the right-hand side of an assignment, the value of the corresponding byte is read from the file:

```
variable = file[index];
```

The syntax is certainly natural — an array of bytes is a common abstract model for a file. The overloading is consistent and complete: The only operation needed is indexing. Unfortunately, these properties are not enough to avoid surprises. Examine Listing 5.1 and see which surprises you can anticipate.

Listing 5.1 Class `FileArray`

```
#include <fstream.h>

class FileArray : public fstream {
    streampos filePtr;
public:
    FileArray(char* fName) :
        fstream(fName, ios::in | ios::out) {}
    FileArray& operator[] (unsigned x);
    FileArray& operator= (char c);
                operator char();
};

FileArray& FileArray::operator[] (unsigned x)
{
    filePtr = streampos(x);
    return *this;
}

FileArray& FileArray::operator= (char buf)
{
    seekp(filePtr, ios::beg);
    write(&buf, 1);
    flush();
    return *this;
}

FileArray::operator char()
{
    char buf;
    seekg(filePtr, ios::beg);
    read(&buf, 1);
    return buf;
}
```

Class `FileArray` is derived from `fstream` and declares `operator[]`, `operator=` and `operator char` to implement an abstraction of a disk file as an array. Class `fstream` supplies operations for reading and writing the file; `fstream` is part of the (de facto) standard Streams class library. The `FileArray` constructor takes a character string as an argument, which it passes to the `fstream` constructor as the name of the file to open. In the second argument to the `fstream` constructor, `ios::in` and `ios::out` are enumerator values defined in class `ios`, which is also part of the Streams library. The value `ios::in|ios::out` specifies that `fstream` should open the file for both input and output. The private `streampos` member of `FileArray` is an index for seeking within an `fstream`. The `streampos` type is also defined in Streams; a `streampos` value corresponds to a position within an `fstream`, used as an argument to functions that seek within files.

To see the operator function members of `FileArray` in action, suppose a program has declared a pair of `FileArray` objects associated, respectively, with a pair of files:

```
FileArray source("input"), dest("output");
char c;
int i, j, n;
```

Although `source` and `dest` can perform both input and output, in the code that follows, `source` will be used only for reading, and `dest` only for writing. If `c` is a `char` variable and `j` an `int` variable, then `c` is assigned the jth character of the `source` file by

```
c = source[j];
```

The reasons that this assignment expression works are not obvious; it is worth following its execution step by step to see exactly what happens. The expression on the right-hand side of the assignment, `source[j]`, is equivalent to `source.operator[](j)`, which converts the value of `j` to a `streampos` and saves the `streampos` value in `source.filePtr`:

```
FileArray& FileArray::operator[] (unsigned x)
{
    filePtr = streampos(x);
    return *this;
}
```

No operation on the file itself has yet been made at this stage in the evaluation of the assignment expression. The `operator[]` function simply saves a `streampos` value and returns a reference-to-`FileArray`, referring to the `this` object, that is, `source`. The types of the operands to the assignment operator are therefore

```
char = FileArray&
```

To satisfy the built-in `char` assignment operator, a conversion must be found that maps the reference-to-`FileArray` on the right-hand side to a `char`. This conversion is exactly what `FileArray::operator char` does. Thus, the entire assignment expression could have been written equivalently as

```
c = (source.operator[](j)).operator char();
```

This form of the expression explicitly shows the overloading rules and conversions that are implicit in the original.

The invocation of the `operator char` conversion is a critical part of the way `FileArray` works:

```
FileArray::operator char()
{
    char buf;
    seekg(filePtr, ios::beg);
    read(&buf, 1);
    return buf;
}
```

It is the conversion operator that reads the underlying file. `FileArray::operator char()` uses `seekg()`, inherited from `fstream` (though originally declared in a further base class, `istream`), to move the read cursor to an offset (relative to the beginning of the file) corresponding to `filePtr`, which still has the value that was set by `operator[]`. Then `read()`, also inherited, reads one byte from that position in the file and returns the value. The returned value is finally assigned to `c` on the left-hand side of the assignment. This completes the explanation of assignment where a `FileArray` object is indexed on the right-hand side.

If the `FileArray` indexing appears on the left-hand side of an assignment expression, the effect must be different — the character in the file must be written, not read. We will now trace the execution of an assignment in which the `FileArray` indexing is on the left-hand side:

```
dest[i] = c;
```

The evaluation of `dest.operator[](i)` for the left-hand side is the same as `source.operator[](j)` was for the right-hand side of the previous assignment. Again, `FileArray::operator[]` merely sets the value of `filePtr` for subsequent use. The assignment operator in this expression, therefore, has operands whose types are reversed from the previous assignment: The reference-to-`FileArray` is on the left and the `char` is on the right:

```
FileArray& = char
```

To satisfy this assignment, `FileArray` must declare an `operator=` for which the `char` on the right can become an argument. Indeed, `FileArray::operator=(char)` matches exactly and is called to perform the assignment. This assignment could have been written equivalently as

```
(dest.operator[](i)).operator=(c);
```

`FileArray::operator=` seeks, writes the character and flushes the file:

```
FileArray& FileArray::operator= (char buf)
{
    seekp(filePtr, ios::beg);
    write(&buf, 1);
    flush();
    return *this;
}
```

The `FileArray` indexing also works, therefore, on the left-hand side of an assignment.

A `FileArray` object can determine the context in which it is being used by virtue of the way its conversion and assignment operators are defined. Very clever! (Maybe even too clever.)

Richer Expressions

Not only can indexing be used on either side of an assignment, it can also be used on both sides of a single assignment to read from one file and write to another:

```
dest[i] = source[j];
```

The indexing is therefore self-consistent; if the overloading let indexing appear only once in an expression, the effect would be unnatural since there is no such prohibition on the indexing of regular arrays. The assignment expression that indexes on both sides is equivalent to

```
(dest.operator[](i)).operator=(
    (source.operator[](j)).operator char()
                        );
```

`FileArray` indexing can also be used naturally in other contexts. Suppose that characters are to be read from one file, converted by a translation table and written to another file. A simple translation table can be implemented as an array of characters:

```
char translate[CHAR_MAX+1];
```

Each character from the input file is mapped through the table and into the output file. The necessary mapping is accomplished by an assignment:

```
dest[i] = translate[ source[j] ];
```

This expression naturally combines `FileArray` indexing with normal array indexing; the two operators interact as expected.

`FileArray` indexing can be combined with other operators in a variety of ways. Three examples follow. First, a character indexed from a `FileArray` object could be used in a relational expression in an `if` statement:

```
if( '_' == source[j] )
    dest[i++] = ' ';
```

Second, a different kind of mapping could be used for a translation table, where 2 is raised to the power of the input character, and the result used to index the table, as follows:

```
dest[i] = translate[ 1 << source[j] ];
```

Third, n insignificant bits (where n is an integer variable) could be shifted out of a character indexed from a file before testing to see if its value is zero:

```
if( source[j] >> n )
    dest[i] = source[j];
```

The expressions above are all legal in C++. The overloading works naturally in all these cases. Or does it? Reread the code. One of the previous three examples of `FileArray` indexing does *not* do what you would expect. Which one holds the surprise, and why?

A Surprise

The surprise is in this example:

```
if( source[j] >> n )
    dest[i] = source[j];
```

The >> operator in `source[j]>>n` does not perform a shift. We must carefully examine each step in the expression's interpretation to see what actually happens.

The left operand of >>, `source[j]`, is equivalent to `source.operator[](j)`, which, as before, returns a reference-to-`FileArray`. The operands for >> are therefore

```
FileArray& >> int
```

`FileArray` does not declare `operator>>`, but it does inherit an `operator>>` from `fstream`. The `operator>>` in `fstream` is in turn inherited from `istream`, two levels higher in the inheritance hierarchy. The significant part of the `FileArray` inheritance hierarchy is shown in Figure 5.1.

There are several overloadings of `operator>>` in `istream`. The one selected in our expression takes a reference-to-`int` argument:

```
class istream : public ios {
public:
// ...
    istream&   operator>>(int&);
// ...
};
```

Figure 5.1 Part of the `FileArray` inheritance hierarchy

This is the familiar >> operator used for reading an integer from a stream, usually invoked as

```
int x;
cin >> x;
```

An equivalent form for source[j]>>n is

```
(source.operator[](j)).istream::operator>>(n)
```

The >> operator has been explained, but the `if` statement has not. The result of an expression in an `if` statement must be either numeric or a pointer. The result returned by istream::operator>>(int&) is a reference-to-istream. Should there not be a compile-time error because the conditional expression is not an arithmetic type nor a pointer type? A reference-to-istream is neither, but there is a conversion from istream to a pointer type. The conversion is defined by ios, the base class of istream:

```
class ios {
public:
// ...
    operator void* ();
// ...
};
```

This conversion operator returns a null pointer if the stream has failed for any reason, and a non-null pointer if all is well. So ios::operator void* converts the reference-to-istream to a pointer-to-void, which the `if` statement can test. The original code in question was

```
if( source[j] >> n )
    dest[i] = source[j];
```

What this code actually means is this: "Read decimal characters from source, starting at the current read position, converting decimal to binary. Save the accumulated value in an integer variable. Then, if the stream has encountered no serious errors, perform the assignment statement." Quite a surprise!

Inheritance for Implementation

Why did this surprise arise and how can it be fixed? The problems stem from inherited operators, rather than the operators defined in `FileArray`. We must ask, therefore, why inheritance is used in the declaration of `FileArray`. Recall an issue raised in Chapter 3: inheritance for interface versus inheritance for implementation. Also recall this rule:

> ▶ **Recognize inheritance for implementation; use a private base class or (preferably) a member object.**

The purpose of a `FileArray` object is to make a disk file look like a character array. The `FileArray` interface is its indexing operators, which realize the abstraction. `FileArray` defines its own interface, getting its implementation from `fstream`. The interface that `FileArray` obtains through public inheritance from `fstream` is redundant. Removing the inheritance removes the extraneous interface. The public inheritance is easily removed by using a private `fstream` object as a member of `FileArray`. As a member object, none of the operations (directly or indirectly) defined by `fstream` is applicable to `FileArray` objects. With the inheritance eliminated, it is easier to understand the behavior of `FileArray`, because all of its behavior is defined in its own class declaration. Listing 5.2 shows `FileArray` rewritten with a member object instead of inheritance.

Listing 5.2 `FileArray` using a member object

```
class FileArray {
    fstream    fs;
    streampos filePtr;
public:
    FileArray(char* fName) :
        fs(fName, ios::in | ios::out) {}
    FileArray& operator[] (unsigned x);
    FileArray& operator= (char c);
            operator char();
};

FileArray& FileArray::operator[] (unsigned x)
{
    filePtr = streampos(x);
    return *this;
}
```

```
FileArray& FileArray::operator= (char c)
{
    fs.seekp(filePtr, ios::beg);
    fs.write(&c, 1);
    fs.flush();
    return *this;
}

FileArray::operator char()
{
    char c;
    fs.seekg(filePtr, ios::beg);
    fs.read(&c, 1);
    return c;
}
```

In the version of class `FileArray` in Listing 5.2, all the original overloaded expressions remain legal. The difference is that now their behavior agrees with their appearance.

Another Surprise

Thus far, all of the expressions involving `FileArray` indexing have had an essential, but unstated, property: Each `FileArray` object has appeared only once in any expression. What happens if the same object is indexed more than once in an expression? Suppose a `FileArray` object called `io` is used for both input and output:

```
FileArray io("input-output");
char c;
int i, j;
```

As long as an intermediate variable is used, copying a character from one position in the file to another behaves as expected:

```
c = io[j];
io[i] = c;
```

Intuitively, the following assignment should be equivalent:

```
io[i] = io[j];
```

Unfortunately, the assignment in which `io` appears on both the left-hand and right-hand sides is not guaranteed to work. It is equivalent to

```
(io.operator[](i)).operator=(
    (io.operator[](j)).operator char()
                    );
```

The critical property of this expression is that it uses `FileArray::operator[]` twice. The `streampos` values corresponding to both `i` and `j` must be saved during the evaluation of the expression. However, `io.filePtr` is the only repository for both pieces of information. Whether or not the expression works depends on its order of evaluation, which is not strictly defined with respect to the way `io.filePtr` is modified. With luck, a compiler might decide to evaluate the whole of the right-hand side of the expression and save the character read from `io[j]`, then evaluate the left-hand index and pass the saved character as an argument to `operator=`. Without such luck, different effects could occur. For example, if both index operations occur before the conversion, the second `operator[]` will overwrite the `filePtr` value saved by the first `operator[]` before that value has been used.

The variations in the generated code can be shown without resorting to reading assembly code. There are four basic steps in the evaluation of

```
io[i] = io[j];
```

The steps are as follows: (1) right-hand side indexing; (2) fetching the character from the right-hand side; (3) left-hand side indexing; and (4) storing the character on the left-hand side. The four steps can be seen by expanding the assignment into four equivalent C++ source statements, using three explicit temporary variables. Typically, a compiler implements such temporary variables using registers. The four statements are

```
FileArray& tempR = io.operator[](j);     // Right
char tempF = tempR.operator char();      // Fetch
FileArray& tempL = io.operator[](i);     // Left
tempL.operator=(tempF);                  // Store
```

If these are written as four separate source statements, the compiler is obliged to evaluate them sequentially. However, when folded into a single source expression, the compiler determines the detailed order of evaluation. The statements above are shown in the order `Right-Fetch-Left-Store`. This is the only order that works — the fetch is performed before the left-hand side indexing overwrites `filePtr`. The other permitted orders of evaluation are `Right-Left-Fetch-Store` and `Left-Right-Fetch-Store`. However, both of these orderings produce incorrect results because `filePtr` is overwritten before its value is used. Only one of the three possible orderings produces the desired result.

Compilers have great latitude in determining both the order of evaluation of expressions and the way side effects of expressions are performed. Therefore, expressions in which a `FileArray` object is indexed more than once may differ in behavior from compiler to compiler, or even differ between different levels of optimization of a single compiler. A bug introduced by depending on the unguaranteed order of evaluation of an expression might emerge only when mature, otherwise reliable code is ported to a new compiler. Such bugs can be extremely frustrating to find.

State

The origins of the second surprise are found if we revisit a central topic of Chapter 2, and consider the state of a `FileArray` object. Why is `filePtr` a member of `FileArray`? In what sense is the value of `filePtr` part of the state of a `FileArray` object?

The logical state of a `FileArray` object is the contents of the file to which it provides access. Between any pair of accesses to a `FileArray` object, the value of `filePtr` is immaterial. The `filePtr` member serves only as a convenient location to save transient information between the execution of `operator[]` and the execution of the subsequent `operator=` or `operator char`. If the executions of two or more indexing operations on a single object are interleaved, a single `filePtr` may be insufficient because the information is not intrinsically part of the `FileArray` object, but is part of each indexing operation. To correct the problem, the `filePtr` information must be moved from `FileArray` itself into an object associated with the indexing.

If the `filePtr` information is placed in another object, there must be one instance of such an object per execution of `FileArray::operator[]`. The lifetime of the object must extend until the `operator=` or `operator char` has had an opportunity to write or read the file, respectively. To operate in this fashion, `FileArray::operator[]` must create an object that is initialized with the position within the file and the identity of the `FileArray` object. The auxiliary object can then carry all the information needed by `operator=` or `operator char`. Let the auxiliary object be of a class called `Index`, since there is one object associated with each index operation. In order to access the index information, `operator=` and `operator char` must be members of `Index`. If `FileArray::operator[]` returns an `Index` object, the pieces all fit. Listing 5.3 shows the source code for this approach.

Listing 5.3 Classes `Index` and `FileArray`

```
class Index {
friend class FileArray;
    FileArray*   fa;
    streampos    filePtr;
                 Index(FileArray* _fa, int x);
public:
    Index&   operator= (char c);
             operator char ();
};

class FileArray {
friend class Index;
    FileArray& operator=(const FileArray &);
    fstream    fs;
public:
    FileArray(char* fName) :
        fs(fName, ios::in | ios::out) {}
    Index operator[] (unsigned x);
};

Index::Index(FileArray* _fa, int x)
{
    fa = _fa;
    filePtr = streampos(x);
}

Index& Index::operator= (char c)
{
    fa->fs.seekp(filePtr, ios::beg);
    fa->fs.write(&c, 1);
    fa->fs.flush();
    return *this;
}

Index::operator char()
{
    char c;
    fa->fs.seekg(filePtr, ios::beg);
    fa->fs.read(&c, 1);
    return c;
}
```

```
Index FileArray::operator[] (unsigned x)
{
    return Index(this, x);
}
```

To understand how `Index` corrects the second surprise, consider

```
io[i] = io[j];
```

once again. The equivalent code with explicit function calls is unchanged:

```
(io.operator[](i)).operator=(
    (io.operator[](j)).operator char()
                        );
```

The difference is that the calls to `io.operator[]` are not returning references to `io`. Each call to `operator[]` creates a temporary `Index` object that records its `FileArray` and offset. The calls to `operator=` and `operator char` are applied to different `Index` objects. Each `Index` object holds its information independently. Any permitted order of evaluation of the expression produces the same result. The expression is equivalent to

```
Index tempi = io.operator[](i);
Index tempj = io.operator[](j);
tempi.operator=(tempj.operator char());
```

This code shows a specific ordering of the creation of the temporary `Index` objects. In the generated code they might be equally well constructed in the reverse order. The behavior of the expression does not depend on the order. There should be no further surprises from using `FileArray`.

By definition, surprises are not obvious. Surprises in operator overloading arise from unexpected interactions of complicated language features. The two surprises that emerged in the original version of `FileArray` have been removed. I believe, but have not proved, that no new ones have been introduced and that no others remain.

A Programming Tradeoff: Overloaded Operators versus Member Functions

The first surprise that arose from the operator overloading in `FileArray` was corrected by simplifying `FileArray`: A member object replaced public inheritance.

However, correcting the second surprise has made the code more complicated: An additional class is needed. Does the notational convenience of writing `file[index]` justify the programming time required to attend to all the details of `FileArray` and `Index`? What does the client code look like if the same abstraction is provided using regular member functions instead of overloaded operators?

Listing 5.4 shows class `ByteFile`. Class `ByteFile` supports the same abstractions as `FileArray` — bytes may be read from or written to a file. The member functions `put()` and `get()` write and read individual bytes, respectively. The significant difference in using member functions is that `ByteFile::put()` can take both the position in the file and the character to be written as explicit arguments. In `FileArray` these two pieces of information are supplied as operands to different operators, and the implementations of those operators are collectively responsible for merging the related information. The implementation of `ByteFile` is trivial by comparison with that of `FileArray`.

Listing 5.4 Class `ByteFile`

```
class ByteFile {
    fstream    fs;
public:
    ByteFile(char* fName) :
        fs(fName, ios::in | ios::out) {}
    void put(unsigned at, char c);
    char get(unsigned at);
};

void ByteFile::put(unsigned at, char c)
{
    fs.seekp(streampos(at), ios::beg);
    fs.write(&c, 1);
    fs.flush();
}

char ByteFile::get(unsigned at)
{
    char c;
    fs.seekg(streampos(at), ios::beg);
    fs.read(&c, 1);
    return c;
}
```

To use `ByteFile` to copy a byte from one file to another, the programmer must write an expression that says exactly which functions to call and how to manipulate their arguments and results. If `source` and `dest` are `ByteFile` objects, we must write the more explicit form

```
dest.put(i, source.get(j));
```

Whether the notational convenience of `FileArray` is worth the effort needed for a correct implementation depends on how much the class is used in terms of the number of times the operations appear in the source of the clients of the abstraction. If input and output operations appear only infrequently in programs, the syntactic convenience of the overloading is negligible, and `ByteFile` is preferred because it is easier to build. If input–output operations pervade the source, the convenience may be a substantial benefit, and the effort to build `FileArray` is warranted. The issue is subjective — a style question for which a simple rule will not suffice.

Summary

The various rules for operator overloading offered at the beginning of the chapter all have the following guideline as their basis:

> ▶ **When overloading operators, avoid surprises.**

We have seen that it takes more than good intentions to apply this rule. In C++, overloaded operators are just one of many language features that determine the meaning and behavior of an expression. The programmer who defines overloaded operators must investigate potential unintended interpretations and find safeguards to protect an unwary client.

Bibliographic Notes

See page 51 of Coplien [1] for an approach to overloading `operator[]` to index a file similar to the classes used in Listing 5.3.

1. Coplien, J. 1992. *Advanced C++ Styles and Idioms*. Reading, MA: Addison-Wesley.
2. Kernighan, B. W., and Plauger, P. J. 1974 (2d ed., 1978). *The Elements of Programming Style*. New York, NY: McGraw-Hill.

Exercises

5.1. For the original `FileArray` in Listing 5.1, what does a=b mean, where a and b are `FileArray` objects?

5.2. Return to Listing 2.5 in Chapter 2. Are the relational operators == and != defined in a complete and consistent fashion?

6

Wrappers

This chapter examines a C++ class that is used as a software layer, or "wrapper," around a utility library written in C. C++ has many features that make it a safer language than C, because in C++ the programmer has to address fewer tedious details. A C++ wrapper class should therefore improve the interface to a library, but the programmer must take care to ensure that this goal is met.

A C Library

The C library that we examine is a collection of functions and structures for interrogating file system directories in the UNIX system. The five C functions are

```
extern "C" {
    DIR      *opendir(char*);
    dirent  *readdir(DIR*);
    long     telldir(DIR*);
    void     seekdir(DIR*, long);
    void     closedir(DIR*);
};
```

DIR and dirent are structures, whose details are of little interest here. The extern "C" qualifying the function prototypes is a *linkage specification,* indicating that the functions are compiled by a C compiler and therefore do not have "mangled" names.

opendir() takes a string argument and attempts to open the named directory so that the contents of the directory may be examined. If the directory is successfully opened, opendir() returns a non-null pointer to a "directory stream," a dynamically allocated instance of `DIR`. The pointer identifies the directory stream in subsequent calls to the other functions. If the open fails for any reason, `opendir()` returns a null pointer. When the client code has finished with the directory stream, it must call `closedir()` to close the directory stream; `closedir()` frees the instance of `DIR`. The pointer must therefore not be used again after the `closedir()` call.

`readdir()` is an *iterator* that delivers entries from the directory stream. For a given `DIR`, each call to `readdir()` returns a pointer to a static instance of `dirent` describing the next entry in the directory. `readdir()` returns a null pointer to mark the end of the iteration when the directory entries are exhausted. A `dirent` structure describes the properties of a directory entry, that is, a file or subdirectory:

```
struct dirent {
    char      d_name[MAXNAMLEN + 1];   /* +1 for \0 */
                                       /* other fields */
};
```

The d_name field of the `dirent` structure is the name of a file or subdirectory (with a terminating null byte). There is other information in a `dirent`, which, for simplicity, we ignore.

`telldir()` returns an index indicating which entry from a directory will be returned on the next call to `readdir()`. A value returned from `telldir()` may be given as an argument to `seekdir()` to reset the iteration to that point. A client may not assume any property of the values returned by `telldir()`; for example, successive values need not even be monotone. The only use a client can make of a value returned by `telldir()` is as an argument to `seekdir()`.

Style Example: A C++ Wrapper for `dirent`

To use this family of C functions, it is important to adhere to all of the conventions — for example, make sure that `closedir()` is called for each directory stream and as the last operation on each stream. A C++ wrapper class can help to manage the housekeeping by encapsulating the pointer-to-`DIR` and using a destructor to guarantee that the call to `closedir()` is performed. A wrapper class, `Directory`, is shown in Listing 6.1.

Listing 6.1 Class `Directory`

```
class Directory {
    DIR     *dir;
public:
            Directory(char*);
            ~Directory();
const char  *name();
    long    tell();
    void    seek(long);
};

Directory::Directory(char *path)
{
    dir = opendir(path);
}

Directory::~Directory()
{
    closedir(dir);
}

const char *Directory::name()
{
    dirent *d = readdir(dir);
    return d ? d->d_name : NULL;
}

long Directory::tell()
{
    return telldir(dir);
}

void Directory::seek(long loc)
{
    seekdir(dir, loc);
}
```

Note that `Directory::name()` returns a pointer to a field of a statically allocated instance of `dirent`. Whenever a function returns a pointer, it is important to establish the *ownership* and lifetime of the object to which it points. In this case a client programmer of `Directory` should know that the character string must be used before the next call to `name()`. To obtain a permanent copy of the string, a client must make its own copy.

The following code, which lists each member of the current working directory, illustrates class `Directory` in action:

```
Directory current(".");
const char *n;
while( n = current.name() )
    printf("%s\n", n);
```

For readers not familiar with the UNIX system, `"."` names the current directory of a process. The `Directory` constructor therefore binds `current` to the current working directory. The advantage of the C++ wrapper class is that there is no need for an explicit call to close the directory stream. The `Directory` destructor is called automatically at the end of the lifetime of `current`, which is on exit from the enclosing block.

The problems with class `Directory` are not apparent from this client code. Under what circumstances does a `Directory` object exhibit unexpected behavior? When does the C++ wrapper impede the programmer of client code? Think about `Directory` objects in more complicated settings and about what might go wrong.

Multiple `Directory` Objects

Suppose the first three entries of each of two directories, called a and b, must be printed side by side. The natural way to use `Directory` for this task is as follows:

```
Directory a("a");
Directory b("b");

for( int i = 1; i <= 3; ++i )
    printf("%s\t%s\n", a.name(), b.name());
```

The output from this code is probably not what you expect. If directory a contains a1, a2, a3, . . . , and directory b contains b1, b2, b3, . . . , the expected output is

```
a1      b1
a2      b2
a3      b3
```

But the actual output is either

```
a1      a1
a2      a2
a3      a3
```

or

```
b1      b1
b2      b2
b3      b3
```

depending on the compiler used.

The root of the problem is the statically allocated instance of `dirent` used by the C function `readdir()`. `Directory::name()` simply passes a pointer to `d->d_name` back to its caller. Any non-null pointer returned by any call to `name()` for any `Directory` object has the same value. C++ client code can instantiate multiple `Directory` objects, but their behavior is not independent, because their implementations share a static character array.

▶ **Know the valid lifetime of a pointer returned from a function.**

The dependence on a static variable can be removed by making `Directory::name()` copy the string to an array declared as a private member of `Directory`. The pointer returned by `name()` should then point to the private copy of the string. See the version of `Directory` in Listing 6.2.

Listing 6.2 `Directory::name()` copies string

```
class Directory {
    DIR     *dir;
    char    nameCopy[sizeof(dirent::d_name)];
public:
            Directory(char*);
            ~Directory();
const char  *name();
    long    tell();
    void    seek(long);
};

Directory::Directory(char *path)
{
    dir = opendir(path);
}

Directory::~Directory()
{
    closedir(dir);
}
```

```
const char *Directory::name()
{
    dirent *d = readdir(dir);
    if( !d )
        return NULL;
    strcpy(nameCopy, d->d_name);
    return nameCopy;
}

long Directory::tell()
{
    return telldir(dir);
}

void Directory::seek(long loc)
{
    seekdir(dir, loc);
}
```

Although the code to print the entries of directories a and b side by side now works correctly, a similar problem remains. The following code does not print the names of the first three entries of directory a:

```
Directory a("a");
printf("%s %s %s\n", a.name(), a.name(), a.name());
```

Instead, it prints three copies of the third entry's name. Each call to a.name() returns a.nameCopy, which contains the third entry's name by the time printf executes. In order to see the first three names, the client programmer must write

```
Directory a("a");
printf("%s ", a.name());
printf("%s ", a.name());
printf("%s\n", a.name());
```

In deciding how to address this issue, the programmer of Directory is faced with a difficult choice. It appears initially to be the same problem as the static string shared by all Directory objects. The solution to that problem was to allocate a character array per object. Perhaps the solution to the current dilemma is to allocate a character array per call to Directory::name(). Character arrays could be allocated on demand using a variety of strategies. If that approach is taken, it is critical to decide whether the Directory object or its client owns the array and is responsible for its deletion.

For class `Directory`, it is reasonable to let the code stand as it is. The client programmer must know that the result from `name()` is good only until the next call to `name()` for that object, and that the client must make copies of strings if it needs more than one at a time. If the client must make a copy of the string, it is clear that the client owns the character array that it allocates.

> ▶ **Independent objects should have independent behavior.**

There is an important difference between this limitation on the use of `Directory::name()` and the original version of `Directory`. In the original `Directory`, the behavior of a `Directory` object could not be understood in isolation. The implementations of all `Directory` objects were merged such that operations on one object could end the validity of a pointer returned by a different object. In the revised version of `Directory`, the client programmer must know the properties of a pointer returned by `Directory::name()`, but those properties depend on only one object.

Constructor Failure

Leaving the question of static character arrays, consider what happens if a directory cannot be opened either because it does not exist or because it does not have appropriate permissions. If a directory called `non-existent` does not exist, the following client code goes astray:

```
Directory current("non-existent");
const char *n;
while( n = current.name() )
    printf("%s\n", n);
```

This code calls `current.name()` even though the `Directory` constructor did not obtain a non-null `DIR` pointer to pass to `readdir`. The behavior of `readdir`, and therefore the behavior of `Directory::name()`, is undefined, causing the program to crash or produce invalid results.

Not only is the client code broken, there is no way to fix it. Whether the constructor succeeded in opening the directory cannot be determined through the public interface to `Directory`. The encapsulation of the pointer-to-`DIR` within `Directory` has completely hidden some information that a client needs in order to use the abstraction effectively.

> ▶ **Do not encapsulate essential information — make it available by some means.**

The `Directory` constructor could detect that `opendir()` has failed, but it is not easy to return status information from a constructor that has run into trouble. Unlike other functions, constructors are called from declarations and may not return a value to the calling context. There are several reasonable approaches to handling failure in constructors, which vary in the way client code interacts with an object in distress. We will examine each of the alternatives in turn.

Robust Failure

The primary goal in handling failure in a constructor, or elsewhere in a class, is *robustness*. The behavior of an object should not be undefined if it is possible to detect the source of the problem and behave predictably. It is better for an object to recognize that things have gone wrong, maintain its own consistency and react predictably than to behave in an undefined fashion. A `Directory` object should detect the failure of `opendir` and handle the event at least reliably, if not gracefully.

The simplest way to deal with failure in `Directory` is to test the pointer-to-`DIR` in the other member functions and never call the C functions with a null pointer argument. The version of `Directory` in Listing 6.3 uses this minimal, but robust, style.

Listing 6.3 Robust failure

```
class Directory {
    DIR     *dir;
    char    nameCopy[sizeof(dirent::d_name)];
public:
            Directory(char*);
            ~Directory();
const char  *name();
    long    tell();
    void    seek(long);
};

Directory::Directory(char *path)
{
    dir = opendir(path);
}
```

```
Directory::~Directory()
{
    if( dir )
        closedir(dir);
}

const char *Directory::name()
{
    if( !dir )
        return NULL;
    dirent *d = readdir(dir);
    if( !d )
        return NULL;
    strcpy(nameCopy, d->d_name);
    return nameCopy;
}

long Directory::tell()
{
    return dir ? telldir(dir) : 0;
}

void Directory::seek(long loc)
{
    if( dir )
        seekdir(dir, loc);
}
```

An object of class `Directory` is now reliable — a directory that cannot be opened appears to be empty. Predictable behavior is indeed better than the undefined behavior of the original code. However, there is no way for a client to distinguish whether an apparently empty directory is a legitimate directory that is empty, or an error. The class has been improved, but is still deficient.

> ▶ **The behavior of an object that has encountered an error should be well-defined.**

Public Access to Failure State

Clients should be able to obtain information about the failure of an object on which they depend. Some clients may not care that there is no distinction between an empty directory and a nondirectory, but most will. We now consider ways to make the failure information accessible to a client. A simple technique is to add a public member function that returns a value indicating an error condition and possibly some details about the error. The version of `Directory` in Listing 6.4 uses this approach.

Listing 6.4 Error member function

```c++
class Directory {
    DIR     *dir;
    char    nameCopy[sizeof(dirent::d_name)];
    char    *errStr;    // NULL => no error
public:
            Directory(char*);
            ~Directory();
const char  *name();
    long    tell();
    void    seek(long);
const char  *error();
};

Directory::Directory(char *path)
{
    errStr = NULL;
    dir = opendir(path);
    if( !dir ){
        if( errno > 0 && errno < sys_nerr )
            errStr = sys_errlist[errno];
        else
            errStr = "unknown error";
        errno = 0;
    }
}

Directory::~Directory()
{
    if( dir )
        closedir(dir);
}

const char *Directory::name()
{
    if( !dir )
        return NULL;
    dirent *d = readdir(dir);
    if( !d )
        return NULL;
    strcpy(nameCopy, d->d_name);
    return nameCopy;
}

long Directory::tell()
{
    return dir ? telldir(dir) : 0;
}
```

```
void Directory::seek(long loc)
{
    if( dir )
        seekdir(dir, loc);
}

const char *Directory::error()
{
    return errStr;
}
```

The version of `Directory` in Listing 6.4 has one additional private data member, `errStr`, and one additional public member function, `error`. As long as a `Directory` object encounters no errors, the value of `errStr` is a null pointer, set at the beginning of the constructor. When a `Directory` object encounters an error (which can only happen in the constructor as the class is now designed), `errStr` is set to point to the text of an error message. The constructor attempts to use the standard UNIX external variables `errno`, `sys_nerr` and `sys_errlist` to build a meaningful message. The `error()` member function returns the current value of `errStr`. A client can detect that there is an error because the return from `error()` is non-null. If the client chooses, the contents of the error message can be reported. The following client code prints an error message if the `Directory` constructor fails:

```
Directory d("/usr/tac");
if( d.error() )
    fprintf(stderr, "error: %s\n", d.error());
```

Under this scheme the client is not obliged to check the error at any particular time. The object records the error and responds to inquiries from the client at the client's convenience.

Error Condition Argument

Listing 6.5 shows another approach to handling failure in the `Directory` constructor. The constructor takes an additional, optional argument, through which the constructor communicates its success or failure.

Listing 6.5 Optional constructor argument

```
class Directory {
    DIR     *dir;
    char    nameCopy[sizeof(dirent::d_name)];
public:
            Directory(char*, int *error = NULL);
            ~Directory();
const char  *name();
    long    tell();
    void    seek(long);
};

Directory::Directory(char *path, int *error)
{
    dir = opendir(path);
    if( error )
        *error = dir ? 0 : 1; // 0 => success
}

Directory::~Directory()
{
    if( dir )
        closedir(dir);
}

const char *Directory::name()
{
    if( !dir )
        return NULL;
    dirent *d = readdir(dir);
    if( !d )
        return NULL;
    strcpy(nameCopy, d->d_name);
    return nameCopy;
}

long Directory::tell()
{
    return dir ? telldir(dir) : 0;
}

void Directory::seek(long loc)
{
    if( dir )
        seekdir(dir, loc);
}
```

If the `error` argument to `Directory::Directory()` is non-null, the constructor sets the value of the corresponding integer to 0 on success and 1 on failure. The following code supplies a non-null pointer, so it can determine if the constructor succeeds:

```
int err;
Directory dot(".", &err);
if( err )
    fprintf(stderr, "error: cannot open .\n");
```

If the client does not provide a second argument, the constructor receives the default value, a null pointer, and ignores the argument:

```
Directory dot(".");
const char *n;
while( n = dot.name() )
    printf("%s\n", n);
```

Note that the optional error argument is a pointer-to-`int`, not a reference-to-`int`. A reference argument would work as well as a pointer if the argument were always required, that is, if there were no default value. A difficulty with an optional reference argument is the choice of a value to designate its absence. A reference must refer to an object; there is no legitimate way to initialize a reference from a null pointer. A reference could be used if a dummy integer existed to serve as the default reference argument. Such an integer could be declared as a static member of `Directory`, as follows:

```
class Directory {
static int   defaultArg;
    DIR      *dir;
    char     nameCopy[sizeof(dirent::d_name)];
public:
             Directory(char*, int &error = defaultArg);
             ~Directory();
const char   *name();
    long     tell();
    void     seek(long);
};

Directory::Directory(char *path, int &error)
{
    dir = opendir(path);
    error = dir ? 0 : 1;
}

int Directory::defaultArg;
```

The constructor always saves the error status in its reference argument. If the argument refers to `defaultArg`, the value is never checked. In this case, it is as simple for the constructor to perform the assignment on every execution as it would be to check whether or not `error` is a client-supplied argument.

Since declaring and defining a static integer member of `Directory` to serve as the default value for a reference argument is somewhat cumbersome, is there any advantage to a reference over a pointer? From the client programmer's perspective, the only difference is that no `&` is prefixed to the actual argument in the calling context:

```
int err;
Directory dot(".", err);
if( err )
    fprintf(stderr, "error: cannot open .\n");
```

Initializer Lists

A second difficulty with an extra argument (whether a pointer or a reference) to constructors arises when the constructor is identified in another constructor's *initializer list*. In the examples used so far, `Directory` objects have been declared in simple declarations. Initializers are required if `Directory` is a base class or if a `Directory` object is a member of another class. To illustrate the problem, consider a font server class that uses `Directory` to find font descriptor files in a given directory. If class `FontServer` has a `Directory` object as a member, then the `FontServer` constructor must have an initializer that supplies arguments to the `Directory` constructor. Ignoring the optional argument to `Directory::Directory()`, class `FontServer` looks like this:

```
class FontServer {
    Directory   fontDir;    // member object
    // ...
public:
        FontServer(char *path);
    // ...
};

FontServer::FontServer(char *path)
    : fontDir(path)                 // initializer
{
    // ...
}
```

If `FontServer` needs to detect whether or not the `Directory` constructor succeeded, it must supply a second argument. What variable is available for use by the `FontServer` initializer as the second argument to the `Directory` constructor? It would be convenient to use an automatic integer variable, but an initializer cannot declare its own automatic variable nor access an automatic variable declared in the body of the constructor. The scope of the constructor body is not entered until the initializers are completed. Therefore, the variable used as the optional argument to the constructor must be statically allocated. A private static member can be used.

```
class FontServer {
    Directory     fontDir;
static int        dirErr;
    // ...
public:
        FontServer(char *path);
    // ...
};

FontServer::FontServer(char *path)
    : fontDir(path, &dirErr)
{
    if( dirErr ){
        // ...
    }
}
```

A single static member is straightforward. Care is needed in more complicated situations to ensure that a single static variable is not used for more than one purpose simultaneously. For example, if `FontServer` had two `Directory` members, it would need two static integers.

Exceptions

Neither the optional constructor argument nor the `error()` member function in Listing 6.4 forces the client programmer to check for failure of a `Directory` object. With such interfaces, the programmer of a server class makes information about errors available in a convenient fashion, to be used at the discretion of the client programmer. Another style of interaction between a server and its clients will become possible when exceptions are added to C++ implementations. If an object encounters an error and throws an exception, its client is forced to catch the exception or lose control as the exception propagates up the function call chain. Of course, using exceptions raises many new questions of programming style, which it is premature to address until we have implementations and some experience. See Chapter 15 of Ellis and Stroustrup for the details about exceptions.

Summary

The original `Directory` wrapper class had two serious flaws. First, the implementation of all `Directory` objects shared a static character array, making the behavior of one object depend on operations applied to another. A character array declared as a member of the class, and therefore instantiated per object, made each object behave autonomously. Second, there was no way to detect whether the wrapper's constructor had failed to open its directory successfully. When faced with an error, `Directory` objects simply misbehaved unpredictably. However, the information about the failure was available from the C library interface. With respect to reporting failure, the C++ wrapper class was a poorer interface than the original C. Several ways have been shown in which the wrapper class might be modified to behave more robustly and communicate errors to its clients. It is hard to say which of the versions in Listings 6.4 and 6.5 is better; they both handle errors in a robust manner with an interface for a client to find out what happened. As with many matters of style, experiment until you find a comfortable compromise and then use it consistently.

> ▶ **Make a C++ wrapper an improvement over the C interface.**

Bibliographic Notes

Ellis, M. A., and Stroustrup, B. 1990. *The Annotated C++ Reference Manual.* Reading, MA: Addison-Wesley.

Exercise

6.1. Class `FileArray` in Chapter 4 is a wrapper. Its `operator[]` hides the details of seeking, reading and writing a disk file. The `FileArray` constructor opens a named file. How does `FileArray` behave if the file cannot be opened?

7

Efficiency

C++ owes much of its popularity to the low-level features, such as in-line functions, that make it possible to write efficient programs. Still, it is often difficult to know when to devote programming effort to matters of efficiency. On the one hand, it is easy to waste time in attempting to optimize a program prematurely, that is, before locating the performance bottlenecks under production conditions. On the other hand, programmers tend to avoid disturbing a debugged class, even if it is the source of performance problems. Programmers must learn to determine which parts of a program require the attention that will make the whole program run efficiently. The skill and judgment to build flexible, efficient software cannot be captured in a few rules of thumb. This chapter serves as a mere introduction to the subject of writing efficient C++ programs.

Regardless of the programming language, it is notoriously difficult to predict the general performance characteristics of a program before running it. The designer of a class makes assumptions, stated and unstated, about how the class will be used by clients. The assumptions are usually about both the frequency of member function calls and the magnitude of the data that the class will typically manipulate. If other programmers use the class in ways that violate these assumptions, serious performance problems may arise. Rectifying such problems involves changing either the implementation of the class or the code of its clients, or both.

Sound encapsulation of a class simplifies the task of changing its implementation in response to performance problems. Strong encapsulation results in low coupling to other classes and reduces the degree to which other parts of the program depend on the implementation algorithms and data structures of a class. Often, an implementation can be replaced with a more efficient one without modifying any client code. By contrast, weak encapsulation makes the task more difficult. The more friends a class has, or the more of its implementation that is public, the harder it is to change the implementation without considering the impact elsewhere.

Some C++ language features assist in writing efficient programs, while careless use of others can cause inefficiencies. For example, declaring a function `inline`, or overloading operators `new` and `delete`, can improve performance dramatically, while the haphazard creation of redundant objects can lead to heavy performance penalties. Not all objects appear explicitly in the source program. The compiler may synthesize temporary objects to serve as function arguments, for example. The language rules that implicitly call for temporary objects obscure execution costs. Source code that looks straightforward may compile into alarmingly expensive machine code.

Style Example: Class `BigInt`

To illustrate some efficiency issues, we will examine class `BigInt` in Listing 7.1. `BigInt` implements non-negative integers of arbitrary length, represented by strings of binary-coded decimal (BCD) digits. A brief explanation of the code may help the reader digest the class more quickly.

The public interface for `BigInt` has three constructors: one for `unsigned`, one for pointer-to-`char`, and a copy constructor. Each of the following declarations creates a `BigInt` with the initial value 123, though a different constructor is used in each case:

```
BigInt a = 123;
BigInt b = "123";
BigInt c = b;
```

The private data members reveal the representation of a `BigInt`: a character string and its length. The character string `digits` is a sequence of BCD digits, without a terminating null byte. In order, `digits[0]` is the least significant and `digit[ndigits-1]` is the most significant. The length, `ndigits`, records the number of digits.

Listing 7.1 Original `BigInt`

```
class BigInt {
    char* digits;
    unsigned ndigits;
    BigInt(char* d, unsigned n) {
        digits = d;
        ndigits = n;
    }
    friend class DigitStream;
public:
    BigInt(const char*);
    BigInt(unsigned n =0);
    BigInt(const BigInt&);
    void operator=(const BigInt&);
    BigInt operator+(const BigInt&) const;
    void print(FILE* f =stdout) const;
    ~BigInt() { delete [] digits; }
};

class DigitStream {
    char* dp;
    unsigned nd;
public:
    DigitStream(const BigInt& n) {
        dp = n.digits;
        nd = n.ndigits;
    }
    unsigned operator++() {
        if (nd == 0) return 0;
        else {
            nd--;
            return *dp++;
        }
    }
};

void BigInt::print(FILE* f) const
{
    for (int i = ndigits-1; i >= 0; i--)
        fprintf(f, "%c", digits[i]+'0');
}

void BigInt::operator=(const BigInt& n)
{
    if (this == &n) return;
    delete [] digits;
    unsigned i = n.ndigits;
    digits = new char[ndigits=i];
    char* p = digits;
    char* q = n.digits;
    while (i--) *p++ = *q++;
}
```

```cpp
BigInt BigInt::operator+(const BigInt& n) const
{
    unsigned maxDigits =
      (ndigits>n.ndigits ? ndigits : n.ndigits)+1;
    char* sumPtr = new char[maxDigits];
    BigInt sum(sumPtr,maxDigits);
    DigitStream a(*this);
    DigitStream b(n);
    unsigned i = maxDigits;
    unsigned carry = 0;
    while (i--) {
        *sumPtr = (++a) + (++b) + carry;
        if (*sumPtr >= 10 ) {
            carry = 1;
            *sumPtr -= 10;
        }
        else carry = 0;
        sumPtr++;
    }
    return sum;
}

BigInt::BigInt(unsigned n)
{
    char d[3*sizeof(unsigned)+1];
    char* dp = d;
    ndigits = 0;
    do {
        *dp++ = n%10;
        n /= 10;
        ndigits++;
    } while (n > 0);
    digits = new char[ndigits];
    for (register i=0; i<ndigits; i++) digits[i] = d[i];
}

BigInt::BigInt(const BigInt& n)
{
    unsigned i = n.ndigits;
    digits = new char[ndigits=i];
    char* p = digits;
    char* q = n.digits;
    while (i--) *p++ = *q++;
}
```

```
BigInt::BigInt(const char* digitString)
{
    unsigned n = strlen(digitString);
    if (n != 0) {
        digits = new char[ndigits=n];
        char* p = digits;
        const char* q = &digitString[n];
        while (n--) *p++ = *--q - '0';
    }
    else {
        digits = new char[ndigits=1];
        digits[0] = 0;
    }
}
```

BigInt has a private constructor and an auxiliary friend class, DigitStream, both used only by BigInt::operator+. Discussing BigInt::operator+ in depth should be sufficient to make the remainder of BigInt self-explanatory. BigInt::operator+ first determines the number of digits in the sum.

```
BigInt BigInt::operator+(const BigInt& n) const
{
    unsigned maxDigits =
        (ndigits>n.ndigits ? ndigits : n.ndigits)+1;
```

The local variable maxDigits is the maximum number of digits that might be needed for the sum string — the number of digits in the longer operand plus one (for possible carry). A local BigInt is needed to accumulate the sum:

```
    char* sumPtr = new char[maxDigits];
    BigInt sum(sumPtr,maxDigits);
```

The sumPtr variable points to a dynamically allocated character string, which is large enough to hold the sum. There is no off-by-one error here; space is not needed for a null byte. The string and its length are the arguments to the private in-line constructor used for sum, a local BigInt. Ownership of the string pointed to by sumPtr is passed to sum. The destructor for sum will delete the string at the end of sum's lifetime, which is upon exit from operator+.

A loop computes the sum by scanning the operands digit by digit, starting with the least significant. In general, the operands will not be of equal length, so the loop must handle exhaustion of either operand after any digit. The auxiliary class, DigitStream, performs the necessary housekeeping:

```
DigitStream a(*this);
DigitStream b(n);
```

`DigitStream` is an iterator: Its in-line `operator++` delivers successive digits from a given `BigInt` object. When the string is exhausted, `DigitStream` pads with zeros, contributing nothing to the sum. Note that the interpretation of `operator++` is specialized to the role of the iterator; it is not the familiar increment operation. For `DigitStream`, `++x` is not related to `x=x+1` and is of questionable value with respect to the consistency criterion discussed in Chapter 5.

The loop that computes the sum is straightforward. After the loop, the sum in hand is returned:

```
unsigned i = maxDigits;
unsigned carry = 0;
while (i--) {
    *sumPtr = (++a) + (++b) + carry;
    if (*sumPtr >= 10 ) {
        carry = 1;
        *sumPtr -= 10;
    }
    else carry = 0;
    sumPtr++;
}
return sum;
```

In the loop, the expression `(++a) + (++b)` does most of the work, extracting digits and checking for exhaustion of the `BigInt` strings. Arithmetic is performed directly on the values from the BCD character strings. The constructors and print function convert strings between ASCII and BCD.

Now consider the interface of `BigInt`. Is the overloading consistent and complete as discussed in Chapter 5? As `BigInt` is defined, it is possible to write `b+i`, but not `i+b`, where `b` is a `BigInt` and `i` is an `unsigned`. `BigInt` is therefore inconsistent. Moreover, `BigInt` defines `+` and `=`, but does not define `+=`. `BigInt` is therefore also incomplete. These issues of consistency and completeness will be addressed later in the chapter.

A matter of style raised by `BigInt::operator=` deserves parenthetic mention: Should the return type of `operator=` be `void`? While there is no restriction on the return type of an overloaded assignment, the prudent choice is a reference to the class type, in this case, `BigInt&`. The `void` return type gratuitously prohibits multiple assignments, such as a = b = c, where a, b and c are of type BigInt. Since it does no immediate harm, let the return type for operator= remain as void.

Study the rest of class BigInt in Listing 7.1. Without spending too much time, speculate on the source of potential performance bottlenecks.

A Simplification

Before we consider the efficiency of BigInt, there is a substantial simplification to make. What purpose does DigitStream serve? Its operator++ member function extracts successive digits from a BigInt, returning zero when the digits are exhausted. DigitStream is very closely coupled to BigInt, forming part of the implementation of BigInt. The coupling is evident in the friend relationship and the BigInt& argument to the DigitStream constructor. DigitStream does not provide a free-standing string manipulation abstraction that might be used elsewhere.

DigitStream is a heavyweight solution to a simple problem. A private member function of BigInt would suffice:

```
class BigInt {
    // ...
    char fetch(int i) const {
        return i < ndigits ? digits[i] : 0;
    }
    // ...
};
```

Given an integer index, fetch() either returns the corresponding digit value or pads with zero. The member function fetch() makes DigitStream redundant. BigInt::operator+ can be rewritten using only fetch(), as shown in Listing 7.2. The difference in performance between DigitStream and fetch() is negligible. In one test, fetch() was marginally faster, but with a different compiler or processor DigitStream might be faster.

The version of BigInt using fetch() is similar to the version using DigitStream. The choice is whether or not to isolate the responsibility for zero-padding in a separate class. Why should fetch() be preferred to DigitStream? The answer is a reduction of coupling. To understand the fetch() version, a programmer needs to look at only one class, rather than at the interaction between two classes. Without DigitStream, there is less coupling in the program. None of the coupling for padding zeros remains, because DigitStream is gone. We have applied a rule first seen in Chapter 4:

▶ **Reduce coupling — minimize interactions between classes.**

"Use a member function instead of a class" would be too simplistic a rule. In other situations, it might be better to create a new class. For example, if `DigitStream` provided a general purpose string management service, for which `BigInt` was one of many clients, it would be natural to capture that service in a separate class. As the situation stands, the operation fits naturally and coherently into `BigInt`.

Listing 7.2 `fetch()` replaces `DigitStream`

```
class BigInt {
    char* digits;
    unsigned ndigits;
    BigInt(char* d, unsigned n) {
        digits = d;
        ndigits = n;
    }
    char fetch(int i) const {
        return i < ndigits ? digits[i] : 0;
    }
public:
    BigInt(const char*);
    BigInt(unsigned n =0);
    BigInt(const BigInt&);
    void operator=(const BigInt&);
    BigInt operator+(const BigInt&) const;
    void print(FILE* f =stdout) const;
    ~BigInt() { delete [] digits; }
};

BigInt BigInt::operator+(const BigInt& n) const
{
    unsigned maxDigits =
      (ndigits>n.ndigits ? ndigits : n.ndigits)+1;
    char* sumPtr = new char[maxDigits];
    BigInt sum(sumPtr,maxDigits);
    unsigned carry = 0;
    for (int i=0; i < maxDigits; ++i) {
        *sumPtr = fetch(i) + n.fetch(i) + carry;
        if (*sumPtr >= 10 ) {
            carry = 1;
            *sumPtr -= 10;
        }
        else carry = 0;
        sumPtr++;
    }
    return sum;
}
```

Exercising `BigInt`

With `DigitStream` replaced by `fetch()`, we turn to questions of efficiency. The performance characteristics of `BigInt` are far from what a casual reading of the code might suggest. A small test reveals that something is wrong:

```
void test()
{
    BigInt b = 1;
    for (int i = 1; i <= 1000; ++i)
        b = b + 1;
}
```

This function initializes a `BigInt` object to the value 1 and then increments it 1,000 times. It takes over six seconds to execute on a 16MHz MC68030 processor, or six milliseconds per increment. Where is the time going?

Clearly, the body of the loop, `b=b+1`, is consuming the time, one way or another. Behind this simple expression is considerable machinery for performing the addition and assignment. Counting the number of dynamically allocated strings provides some measure of the amount of work involved. Each execution of the expression `b=b+1` allocates four strings. The right-hand operand of + is an integer, requiring the creation of a temporary `BigInt` object to match the argument type of `operator+`. The constructor for that temporary `BigInt` object allocates the first string. Then `operator+` itself allocates the second string, for `sumPtr`. The value returned from `operator+` is another `BigInt` object, created by applying the copy constructor to `sum` in the `return` statement. The copy constructor allocates the third string. Finally, `operator=` allocates the fourth string. Each string should also be deleted, resulting in a total of eight calls to the memory allocator on every iteration. Could those eight calls account for the observed six milliseconds per iteration? Perhaps a special-purpose memory allocator would solve the performance problem.

Dynamic string allocation may be *a* performance problem, but we should make sure we have identified *the* problem before we seek a specific solution. An execution profiler will show if the memory allocator is consuming the majority of the processor. Execution profile results are shown in the Table 7.1, listing the greediest functions in descending order of their consumption of the processor. Functions consuming less than one percent of the processor are not shown.

Table 7.1 Execution Profile of `test()`

Function	% of time
`BigInt::operator+`	57
`BigInt::operator=`	19
`BigInt::BigInt(BigInt&)`	19
`malloc`	2
`free`	1

Memory allocator functions (`malloc` and `free`) barely squeeze in at the end of the Table; they are not responsible for the poor performance. The member functions of `BigInt` are consuming 95 percent of the processor; `operator+` alone accounts for over 50 percent.

▶ **Don't guess. Use an execution profiler to isolate performance problems.**

Introducing a special-purpose memory allocator cannot help performance significantly. If the memory allocator were taking all the processor left by `BigInt`, and all that overhead could be eliminated, the gain would be only about five percent. We must discover why the `BigInt` member functions are consuming so much of the processor.

The Length of Dynamic Strings

An important clue is that four member functions of `BigInt` participate in each execution of `b=b+1`, but only three appear at the top of the execution profile. The fourth function, `BigInt::BigInt(unsigned)`, appears far down the list, consuming a negligible 0.3 percent of the processor. This constructor executes as often as the other functions and has two non-trivial loops. The difference is that its iteration is governed by the magnitude of its argument (always 1), whereas iteration in the others is governed by the current length of the `BigInt` string. Ironically, `BigInt::BigInt(unsigned)` has a `register` variable (the only one in `BigInt`) controlling the second loop. The `register` variable suggests some concern for the efficiency of `BigInt`, but the number of iterations of the loop is always bounded by the maximum number of decimal digits in an unsigned integer. The statement before the loop always executes `new`, a relatively expensive operation, which must dominate the function overall. The `register` declaration can have no impact on the performance of `BigInt`.

How do the lengths of strings in `BigInt` grow? After the loop in `test()`, `b` should have the value 1,001, requiring 4 bytes. How many bytes are allocated? The length of the string grows only in `operator+`, when `maxDigits` is determined. Here is the problem: `maxDigits` always contains room for a carry digit in the most significant place, even when not needed. When there is no carry, `operator+` adds a leading zero. By the end of the loop in `test()`, `b` has 997 leading zeros before 4 significant decimal digits, 1001. The program spends most of its time manipulating long strings of zeros.

In class `BigInt`, both the numeric value of a number and the way it is computed determine the amount of space it occupies. The implementation is written under the implicit assumption that `operator+` will be used infrequently. If `BigInt` were used mainly for storing numbers, and only rarely for performing arithmetic, there would be no performance problem.

More abstractly, we should distinguish between the *logical state* and *physical state* of a `BigInt` object. As explained in Chapter 2, the logical state of an object is its state as viewed by a client through the public interface. The logical state determines the object's future behavior as it can be observed through the public interface. The physical state of an object is the state of the data structures that represent it. In `BigInt`, a single logical numeric value can be represented by an unbounded set of physical states. For example, the logical state corresponding to the numeric value 123 can be represented by the physical states 123, 0123, 00123, and so on.

A class designer must take extra care when more than one physical state corresponds to a single logical state. For example, to add `operator==` to `BigInt`, the comparison must reflect the logical state rather than the physical state. Simply comparing the `digits` strings for equality would result in 123 being unequal to 0123. We see a similar problem in `BigInt::print()`, where all the leading zeros are output. The following code displays 006 rather than just 6:

```
BigInt a = 1;
a = a + 2;
a = a + 3;
a.print();
```

The performance problem in `BigInt` is that the lengths of dynamic strings are growing without bound. There is a simple correction: `operator+` should *normalize* the sum before returning its result, which means removing a leading zero if introduced by the arithmetic. After the addition in `operator+`, it is easy to recognize that there was no carry into the most significant digit and decrement `sum.ndigits`. The normalization must examine the most significant character in `sum`. The needed code is

```
if (sum.digits[maxDigits-1] == 0)
    --sum.ndigits;
```

Listing 7.3 shows `operator+` with the normalization code incorporated. If we repeat the timing test to see the performance improvement, the execution time for `test()` has dropped from 6 seconds to 0.37 seconds, more than a factor of 16. Such a dramatic performance improvement is not often won so easily and would usually signal a task completed. More often, many small gains are achieved incrementally, as the cycle of instrumentation and modification is repeated. To learn more about `BigInt`, we will search for further improvements.

Listing 7.3 `operator+` **normalized**

```
BigInt BigInt::operator+(const BigInt& n) const
{
    unsigned maxDigits =
      (ndigits>n.ndigits ? ndigits : n.ndigits)+1;
    char* sumPtr = new char[maxDigits];
    BigInt sum(sumPtr,maxDigits);
    unsigned carry = 0;
    for (int i=0; i < maxDigits; ++i) {
        *sumPtr = fetch(i) + n.fetch(i) + carry;
        if (*sumPtr >= 10 ) {
            carry = 1;
            *sumPtr -= 10;
        }
        else carry = 0;
        sumPtr++;
    }
    if (sum.digits[maxDigits-1] == 0)
        --sum.ndigits;
    return sum;
}
```

The Number of Dynamic Strings

We determined earlier that each iteration in `test()` allocates four strings. Has memory allocation now become the dominant consumer of processor time? Table 7.2 shows the new execution profile.

Table 7.2 Execution Profile with Normalization in `operator+`

Function	% of time
`malloc`	27
`free`	22
`BigInt::operator+`	14
`::operator delete`	8
`BigInt::BigInt(BigInt&)`	7
`BigInt::operator=`	6
`::operator new`	5

As originally suspected, the memory allocation routines, with three of the top four functions in the profile, do dominate now, taking 62 percent of the processor.

The better we understand the exact behavior of a program, the easier it is to improve its performance. It now makes sense to instrument the memory allocation activity more precisely. Overloading the global operators `new` and `delete` to gather statistics will show the number of allocated strings. We require versions of operators `new` and `delete` that count every call, but otherwise manage memory in the normal fashion. A simple class *module,* `HeapStats`, encapsulates the counters for `new` and `delete` together with functions for printing and resetting the counters, shown in Listing 7.4. The statistics from `HeapStats` are crude, but provide a wealth of information.

Listing 7.4 Module `HeapStats`

```
class HeapStats {               // module
friend void* operator new(size_t);
friend void  operator delete(void*);
static int  newN;       // # of calls to operator new
static int  deleteN;    // # of calls to operator delete
public:
static void report(FILE *f = stdout);
static void reset();
};

int HeapStats::newN = 0;
int HeapStats::deleteN = 0;

void HeapStats::report(FILE *f)
{
    fprintf(f, "%d operator new calls\n", newN);
    fprintf(f, "%d operator delete calls\n", deleteN);
    fflush(f);
}
```

```
void HeapStats::reset()
{
    newN = 0;
    deleteN = 0;
}

void *operator new(size_t sz)    // statistics and malloc()
{
    ++HeapStats::newN;
    return malloc(sz);
}

void operator delete(void* p)    // statistics and free()
{
    ++HeapStats::deleteN;
    free(p);
}
```

Class `HeapStats` is referred to as a module because its purpose is different than that of regular classes. A class usually serves as a type from which objects are instantiated. `HeapStats` contains only static members, so there is no point in instantiating an object from it. The purpose of `HeapStats` is simply to collect and encapsulate the static members in a single scope. What would otherwise be a collection of global variables and nonmember functions have been given a common identity as members of a single class. Modules make programs more manageable by improving organization and enforcing encapsulation. Modules also reduce the competition for global names in a large program, because each module needs only one global name, not a global name for each member.

Surrounding a call to `test()` with calls to `HeapStats` generates the needed statistics:

```
HeapStats::reset();
test();
HeapStats::report();
```

`test()` remains intact from its previous usage:

```
void test()
{
    BigInt b = 1;
    for (int i = 1; i <= 1000; ++i)
        b = b + 1;
}
```

The output from `HeapStats` is

```
4001 operator new calls
4001 operator delete calls
```

First, notice that there is no memory leak: The number of calls to `new` equals the number of calls to `delete`. If the program had a memory leak, `HeapStats` could be used to identify the problem by monitoring different parts in isolation. Of the 4,001 allocations, the loop accounts for 4,000. The constructor and destructor for `b` itself account for the remaining one.

If there is no way to avoid the dynamic allocation of so many strings, performance might be improved by designing a special-purpose memory allocator for `BigInt`. Before pursuing that path, let us look for ways to reduce the demand for dynamic strings. The four string allocations per iteration are due partly to the implementation of `BigInt`, and partly to the way the expression b=b+1 is written.

In the implementation of `BigInt`, the string deallocation and reallocation by `operator=` is usually unnecessary. As it stands, `operator=` always allocates anew, even if the old string is already the correct size. If the sizes match, there is no need to delete the old string and allocate another. An optimized version of `operator=` is shown in Listing 7.5. The optimization will not improve every program that uses `BigInt`. Those programs in which most assignments are between numbers of different sizes will not benefit. Still, the cost of determining that the optimization cannot be applied is negligible: an additional, but very cheap, integer comparison before the relatively expensive string allocation.

Listing 7.5 `operator=` optimized

```
void BigInt::operator=(const BigInt& n)
{
    if (this == &n) return;
    unsigned i = n.ndigits;
    if (ndigits != i){
        delete [] digits;
        digits = new char[i];
    }
    ndigits=i;
    char* p = digits;
    char* q = n.digits;
    while (i--) *p++ = *q++;
}
```

In 997 of the 1,000 assignments executed by `test()`, the left-hand side is the correct size, and the optimization works. `HeapStats` shows 997 fewer allocations.

```
3004 operator new calls
3004 operator delete calls
```

The time to execute `test()` drops by another 13 percent to 0.32 seconds (from 0.37 seconds). Given the depth of analysis and the amount of programming involved, 13 percent is closer to a typical improvement than the remarkable factor of 16 obtained in the first modification.

None of the changes to `BigInt` has affected its public interface. There was no need to change the client code, because only the encapsulated details of `BigInt` were involved. The client code does provide information about the pattern of use that `BigInt` is experiencing, but there is no need to adjust the client code to implement the performance improvements. This is encapsulation at work.

> ► **Look in class implementations for the source of performance problems.**

This rule applies equally well to classes that do not use operator overloading. The overloading changes the syntax by which a client communicates with objects, but not the principles of building efficient programs.

The Client Code

The modifications so far have all been made to the implementation of `BigInt`. Modifications to the client, `test()`, can also improve performance. The critical statement in `test()` is

```
b = b + 1;
```

The treatment of the literal `1` under the overloading of the `+` operator is different from that of a regular arithmetic expression. As described above, the `1` becomes an argument to the constructor for a temporary `BigInt` object, which is passed by reference to `operator+`. The following loop is equivalent to the body of `test()`:

```
for (int i = 1; i <= 1000; ++i){
    BigInt one = 1;
    b = b + one;
}
```

A C++ compiler is not free to optimize this code by moving the declaration of the temporary object outside the loop. The implementation of `BigInt` cannot tell what is happening; it must handle each member function call in isolation. The programmer of the loop must recognize the creation of the temporary `BigInt` object and decide to move it out of the loop explicitly. The loop can be rewritten as:

```
void test()
{
    BigInt b = 1;
    const BigInt one = 1;
    for (int i = 1; i <= 1000; ++i)
        b = b + one;
}
```

With that change to `test()`, the report from `HeapStats` confirms that one more allocation per iteration has been eliminated:

```
2005 operator new calls
2005 operator delete calls
```

The modified version of `test()` takes 0.23 seconds, down another 28 percent from the original version, and down by a factor of about 25 from the original versions of `test()` and `BigInt`.

The performance of a C++ program depends on both the implementation of its classes and the coding of the clients of those classes. In this case the client unnecessarily created a temporary object whose constructor allocates a string dynamically. The responsibility for knowing the relative costs of different operations falls on the programmer of the client code. If efficiency is important, the client programmer must understand the costs of using a class. In this program, the advantage of operator overloading — natural and terse notation — is offset by the difficulty of determining the costs.

▶ **Look in client code for the source of performance problems.**

Again, there is nothing specific to operator overloading in this rule; it applies equally well to classes that do not use operator overloading.

Table 7.3 Execution Profile of Revised `test()`

Function	% of time
BigInt::operator+	26
malloc	23
free	17
BigInt::BigInt(BigInt&)	10
BigInt::operator=	9
::operator delete	6
::operator new	5

The execution profile for the revised `test()` is shown in Table 7.3. `BigInt` and memory allocation now take similar proportions of the processor: 45 percent and 51 percent, respectively.

Rewriting `BigInt`

Careful reimplementation of `BigInt` can further improve the overall efficiency of `test()`. As `BigInt` stands, two string allocations are performed in each iteration of the loop in `test()`. Two techniques can be applied to `BigInt`, each of which eliminates one string allocation on almost every iteration, resulting in an even faster program.

We noted earlier that `BigInt` was both inconsistent and incomplete. The inconsistency and incompleteness of `BigInt` should also be addressed. For consistency, both `b+i` and `i+b` should be permitted, where `b` is a `BigInt` and `i` is an `unsigned`. To achieve this commutativity, `operator+` should become a nonmember operator function taking two `BigInt` arguments:

```
BigInt operator+(const BigInt& left, const BigInt& right)
```

As a member operator function, the left operand of `+` had to be a `BigInt` object. When `operator+` is a nonmember function, conversions are applied to both arguments, so the left operand can be of any type for which there is conversion to `BigInt`, in particular, `unsigned+BigInt` will work.

To address the incompleteness of `BigInt`, `operator+=` should be added. If `operator+=` is implemented independently of `operator+`, almost the same arithmetic code will appear in each function. Because the operators are related, it should be possible to implement one in terms of the other. It seems natural to implement += in terms of + and =, since += is defined in terms of + and =, but that turns out to be inefficient. The natural implementation is

```
BigInt& BigInt::operator+=(const BigInt& rhs)
{
    return *this = *this + rhs;
}
```

Although this code is correct, it must create at least one temporary BigInt object for the return value from operator+. Given that the += operator modifies an existing value, it would be better to find an implementation that only allocates a string in the case where the memory needed for the BigInt being modified has to grow.

The alternative is to implement operator+= as the primitive operation and then implement operator+ (now a nonmember function) in terms of operator+=. The most straightforward implementation of operator+ in terms of operator+= is

```
BigInt operator+(const BigInt& left, const BigInt& right)
{
    BigInt sum = left;
    return sum += right;
}
```

This version of operator+ creates as many objects as the original operator+ — sum and the returned object. The value returned from operator+ must be a BigInt, so there is no way to avoid creating one BigInt object. But is sum necessary? The local object, sum, can indeed be eliminated by moving all of the work of operator+ into a special-purpose private constructor, an *operator constructor.* An operator constructor performs all the work that logically belongs in an operator. The corresponding operator function contains only a return statement that uses the operator constructor to build the returned object. In this case we need an operator constructor that directly constructs a BigInt object that is the sum of two others. All operator+ needs to do is return an object initialized by the operator constructor:

```
inline
BigInt operator+(const BigInt& left, const BigInt& right)
{
    return BigInt(left, right);
}
```

The operator constructor copies the value of the first argument (the left operand of the +) and then uses `operator+=` to perform the arithmetic.

```
BigInt::BigInt(const BigInt& left, const BigInt& right)
{
    size = 1+(left.ndigits > right.ndigits
                ? left.ndigits : right.ndigits);
    digits = new char[size];
    ndigits = left.ndigits;
    for (int i = 0; i < ndigits; ++i)
        digits[i] = left.digits[i];
    *this += right;
}
```

Note the introduction of `size`. In addition to `ndigits`, the revised version of `BigInt` has a member that records the number of bytes in the `digits` character array. As before, `ndigits` records the number of digits actually being used.

`BigInt::operator+=` performs the arithmetic. It must determine the maximum length of its result, allocate a new string if necessary, and normalize the result. The entire revised version of `BigInt` is shown in Listing 7.6.

Listing 7.6 Class `BigInt` revised

```
class BigInt {
    char* digits;
    unsigned ndigits;
    unsigned size;          // size of allocated string
    BigInt(const BigInt&, const BigInt&);   // + ctor
    char fetch(int i) const;
public:
    BigInt(const char*);
    BigInt(unsigned = 0);
    BigInt(const BigInt&);
    BigInt& operator=(const BigInt&);
    BigInt& operator+=(const BigInt &);
friend BigInt operator+(const BigInt&, const BigInt&);
    void print(FILE* = stdout) const;
    ~BigInt();
};

BigInt::~BigInt()
{
    delete [] digits;
}
```

```
inline
char BigInt::fetch(int i) const
{
    return i < ndigits ? digits[i] : 0;
}


inline
BigInt operator+(const BigInt& left, const BigInt& right)
{
    return BigInt(left, right);
}


BigInt& BigInt::operator+=(const BigInt& rhs)
{
    unsigned max = 1+(rhs.ndigits > ndigits
                            ? rhs.ndigits : ndigits);
    if (size < max){
        char *d = new char[size = max];
        for (int i = 0; i < ndigits; ++i )
            d[i] = digits[i];
        delete [] digits;
        digits = d;
    }
    while (ndigits < max)
        digits[ndigits++] = 0;
    for (int i=0; i<ndigits; ++i){
        digits[i] += rhs.fetch(i);
        if (digits[i] >= 10){
            digits[i] -= 10;
            digits[i+1] += 1;
        }
    }
    if (digits[ndigits-1] == 0)
        --ndigits;
    return *this;
}


void BigInt::print(FILE* f) const
{
    for (int i = ndigits-1; i >= 0; i--)
        fprintf(f, "%c", digits[i]+'0');
}
```

```cpp
BigInt& BigInt::operator=(const BigInt& rhs)
{
    if (this == &rhs) return *this;
    ndigits = rhs.ndigits;
    if (ndigits > size){
        delete [] digits;
        digits = new char[size=ndigits];
    }
    for (int i = 0; i < ndigits; ++i)
        digits[i] = rhs.digits[i];
    return *this;
}

BigInt::BigInt(const BigInt& left, const BigInt& right)
{
    size = 1+(left.ndigits > right.ndigits
                ? left.ndigits : right.ndigits);
    digits = new char[size];
    ndigits = left.ndigits;
    for (int i = 0; i < ndigits; ++i)
        digits[i] = left.digits[i];
    *this += right;
}

BigInt::BigInt(unsigned u)
{
    unsigned v = u;
    for (ndigits = 1; (v/=10) > 0; ++ndigits)
        ;
    digits = new char[size=ndigits];
    for (int i = 0; i < ndigits; ++i){
        digits[i] = u%10;
        u /= 10;
    }
}

BigInt::BigInt(const BigInt& copyFrom)
{
    size = ndigits = copyFrom.ndigits;
    digits = new char[size];
    for (int i = 0; i < ndigits; ++i)
        digits[i] = copyFrom.digits[i];
}

BigInt::BigInt(const char* string)
{
    if( string[0] == '\0' ) // treat "" as "0"
        string = "0";
    size = ndigits = strlen(string);
    digits = new char[size];
    for (int i = 0; i < ndigits; ++i)
        digits[i] = string[ndigits-1-i]-'0';
}
```

To see that the operator constructor reduces the number of `BigInt` objects, we must execute `test()` against the version of `BigInt` in Listing 7.6. As modified to use an explicit constant `BigInt` object for the constant 1, the `test()` function is

```
void test()
{
    BigInt b = 1;
    const BigInt one = 1;
    for (int i = 1; i <= 1000; ++i)
        b = b + one;
}
```

Because `operator+` uses its operator constructor to construct its returned object, only one string is allocated per execution of b=b+one in `test()`. For the entire execution of `test()`, only about 1,000 strings are needed:

```
1005 operator new calls
1005 operator delete calls
```

The time to execute `test()` using the revised `BigInt` is 0.15 seconds. This improvement came from the implementation of `BigInt`.

Performance can also be improved by modifying `test()` once more. Instead of using + and = to increment b, `test()` could use the += operator. The `BigInt` interface has been completed by the addition of +=. To improve efficiency, a client should use += when appropriate:

```
void test()
{
    BigInt b = 1;
    const BigInt one = 1;
    for (int i = 1; i <= 1000; ++i)
        b += one;
}
```

This version of `test()` only allocates a string when the size of the string has to grow, which rarely happens. The total string allocations are reduced to six:

```
6 operator new calls
6 operator delete calls
```

The version of `test()` using `operator+=` executes in 0.033 seconds, allocating 6 strings. Recall that the original `test()` and `BigInt` took 6 seconds and allocated 4,000 strings.

► **A complete interface invites efficient client code.**

Once again the rule is applicable to classes that do not use operator overloading. With operator overloading it is relatively easy to decide when a class is complete. For an interface defined by a set of public member functions, completeness is more subjective. In general, a richer interface with specialized services can be exploited more efficiently by clients than can a minimal interface. This advice is at odds with a rule from Chapter 3 that argues for simplicity in interfaces.

► **Look for simple abstractions.**

The tension between these two rules often calls for compromise. The best approach is to defer considerations of efficiency until information about which classes are performance bottlenecks is available. Many efficiency issues cannot be addressed until classes have been exercised in (perhaps simulated) production settings. This argues for designing class interfaces that are initially simple, but that grow with accumulated experience of their use.

Another Measure

The performance improvement between the original `BigInt` and the revised version is exaggerated by `test()`. The function performs only the `+=` operation. A more realistic measure of the difference between the implementations of `BigInt` should be obtained from a function that performs a mixture of assignments and arithmetic. Although far from a comprehensive benchmark for `BigInt`, the following function is a better measure than `test()`; it computes the 1,000th Fibonacci number by iteration:

```cpp
BigInt fib()
{
    BigInt a=1, b=1, c;
    for (int i = 3; i <= 1000; ++i){
        c = a + b;
        a = b;
        b = c;
    }
    return c;
}
```

Using the original implementation of `BigInt`, `fib()` requires 10.5 seconds. With the revised version of `BigInt`, it runs in 2.0 seconds.

Summary

With respect to writing efficient programs, C++ is much like other programming languages. The first step towards improved performance must be the identification of performance bottlenecks under production conditions. In correcting performance problems, C++ differs from many languages because classes encapsulate their implementations, denying implementation-dependent shortcuts to clients. Having identified the causes of poor performance, there are three techniques for increasing efficiency. First, performance may be improved by modifying the encapsulated implementation, in which case client code is unaffected. Second, the client code may be changed to use an existing interface more efficiently. Third, the interface itself may be at fault, calling for modification of both the class and its clients. In some cases, optimal results may be obtained only if all three techniques are used.

Bibliographic Notes

Efficient programming follows from understanding the properties of algorithms and data structures, and how they are mapped into code. Bentley [1] provides a wealth of practical advice on the subject, most of which is applicable to writing efficient C++ programs.

1. Bentley, J. 1982. *Writing Efficient Programs.* Englewood Cliffs, NJ: Prentice-Hall.

Exercises

7.1. Can the performance of `fib()`, using the version of `BigInt` from Listing 7.6, be improved? Hint: Can `fib()` be rewritten in terms of +=?

7.2. `BigInt` uses BCD as its representation of integers. How does its performance change if the underlying base is changed from 10 to 100? What other bases might be used?

7.3. Class `BigInt` in Listing 7.6 has only one operator constructor. If a second operator constructor were needed that took the same number and types of arguments as the original (say, for binary –), how might the resulting ambiguity be resolved?

8

A Case Study

There has been a central theme to each of the previous chapters. For example, Chapter 2 focused on consistency, and Chapter 7 concentrated on efficiency. This chapter has no such theme. Instead, this chapter studies one program in depth, rewriting it several times with incremental corrections. The goal is to find a better expression in C++ of the programmer's original design. Style rules from previous chapters are applied where appropriate, and some new rules also arise.

Style Example: Finite State Machines

The program in question implements a *finite state machine,* or FSM. An FSM is an abstract machine that at any time is in exactly one of its finite set of states. When it receives an input character, an FSM makes a "transition," changing to another state. The state after the transition (which may be the same as the one before the transition) depends only on the current state and the current input character. An FSM is a powerful tool for building software for recognizing sequences of tokens that match simple patterns, such as a lexical scanner for a compiler.

Any FSM can be described by a transition graph. Each node in the graph corresponds to a state in the machine. Each directed edge in the graph corresponds to the transition from one state to another that occurs when the input character matches that edge's label. Figure 8.1 shows the transition graph for the FSM in the program studied here.

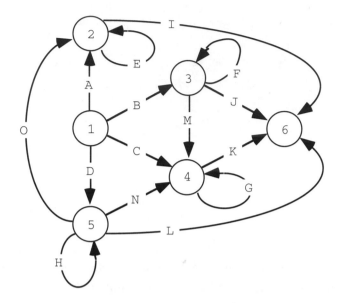

Figure 8.1 FSM transition graph

The finite state machine has six states. If the FSM is in state number 1 and the input character is an "A," the transition is to state number 2. If the next input is an "E," the FSM remains in state 2. From state 2, only an "I" can move it to a different state, number 6. If there is no edge corresponding to the current state and current input character, the FSM goes to a special "doom state" (not shown in the graph), in which it remains under all further inputs. Two of the states in the graph are also special: State 1 is the "start state," the machine's initial state, and state 6 is the "end state," which indicates the successful recognition of an input string.

To drive an FSM, it must be put in its start state and fed a sequence of characters. The FSM must eventually reach either the end state or the doom state. (If the input sequence is exhausted, the FSM goes to the doom state.) If the FSM reaches the end state before the doom state, it accepts the input sequence; if the FSM reaches the doom state first, it rejects the sequence.

Readers familiar with finite state machines will notice a restriction to the established model. The model used here is that chosen by the original programmer of the code to be studied. The machine accepts an input sequence immediately upon entering the end state. There are no further transitions from the end state. In the usual model, a subset of the states is designated the "accepting states"; the machine can undergo a transition from an accepting state to another state; and the final state determines whether or not an input is accepted. The usual model also permits the start state to be an accepting state, so that an empty input sequence can be accepted.

Listing 8.1 shows a program for the finite state machine corresponding to the transition graph in Figure 8.1. Take some time to read it and decide how you might improve it.

Listing 8.1 Original FSM program

```
#include <string.h>

struct parent
{
    static char* expression;
    static index;
    static end_state;    // 1 when last state is reached, 0
                         // otherwise
    static doom_state;   // 1 when illegal input occurs, 0
                         // otherwise
    parent( char* expr );
    virtual parent* transition() {}
};

parent::parent( char* expr )
{
    expression = new char[ strlen( expr ) ];
    strcpy( expression, expr );
    end_state = 0;
    doom_state = 0;
    index = 0;
}

struct state1 : public parent
{
    parent *ptr2, *ptr3, *ptr4, *ptr5;
    state1() : parent( expression ) {}
    parent* transition();
};
```

```
struct state2 : public parent
{
    parent *ptr2;
    state2() : parent( expression ) {}
    parent* transition();
};

struct state3 : public parent
{
    parent *ptr3, *ptr4;
    state3() : parent( expression ) {}
    parent* transition();
};

struct state4 : public parent
{
    parent *ptr4;
    state4() : parent( expression ) {}
    parent* transition();
};

struct state5 : public parent
{
    parent *ptr2, *ptr4, *ptr5;
    state5() : parent( expression ) {}
    parent* transition();
};

parent* state1::transition()
{
    switch( expression[ index++ ] )
    {
        case 'A':
            return ptr2;
        case 'B':
            return ptr3;
        case 'C':
            return ptr4;
        case 'D':
            return ptr5;
        case '\0':
            doom_state = 1;
        default:
            doom_state = 1;
    }
}
```

```
parent* state2::transition()
{
    switch( expression[ index++ ] )
    {
        case 'E':
            return ptr2;
        case 'I':
            end_state = 1;
            break;
        case '\0':
            doom_state = 1;
        default:
            doom_state = 1;
    }
}

parent* state3::transition()
{
    switch( expression[ index++ ] )
    {
        case 'F':
            return ptr3;
        case 'M':
            return ptr4;
        case 'J':
            end_state = 1;
            break;
        case '\0':
            doom_state = 1;
        default:
            doom_state = 1;
    }
}

parent* state4::transition()
{
    switch( expression[ index++ ] )
    {
        case 'G':
            return ptr4;
        case 'K':
            end_state = 1;
            break;
        case '\0':
            doom_state = 1;
        default:
            doom_state = 1;
    }
}
```

```
parent* state5::transition()
{
    switch( expression[ index++ ] )
    {
        case 'O':
            return ptr2;
        case 'H':
            return ptr5;
        case 'L':
            end_state = 1;
            break;
        case 'N':
            return ptr4;
        case '\0':
            doom_state = 1;
        default:
            doom_state = 1;
    }
}

char* parent::expression = NULL;
int parent::doom_state = 0;
int parent::end_state = 0;
int parent::index = 0;

state1 s1;
state2 s2;
state3 s3;
state4 s4;
state5 s5;

void build_state_machine()
{
    s1.ptr2 = &s2;
    s1.ptr3 = &s3;
    s1.ptr4 = &s4;
    s1.ptr5 = &s5;
    s2.ptr2 = &s2;
    s3.ptr3 = &s3;
    s3.ptr4 = &s4;
    s4.ptr4 = &s4;
    s5.ptr2 = &s2;
    s5.ptr4 = &s4;
    s5.ptr5 = &s5;
}

#include <stdio.h>
```

```
main()
{
    build_state_machine();
    char input_string[80];
    printf("Enter input expression: ");
    scanf("%s", input_string);
    parent state_machine(input_string);
    parent *ptr;
    ptr = s1.transition();
    while( ptr->end_state != 1 && ptr->doom_state != 1 )
    {
        ptr = ptr->transition();
    }
    if( ptr->end_state == 1 )
        printf("\nValid input expression");
    else
        printf("\nInvalid input expression");
    return 0;
}
```

Initialization

States 1 through 5 in the transition graph correspond to the structures `state1` through `state5` and the global objects `s1` through `s5`. The structures share a common base class, `parent`, as shown in Figure 8.2. Declaration as `struct` instead of `class` does not prevent inheritance. The main distinction between structures and classes is that, by default, members of a structure are public, whereas members of a class are private. Member functions, constructors, inheritance, and so forth, although usually associated with classes, work equally well with structures (see Ellis and Stroustrup, page 165).

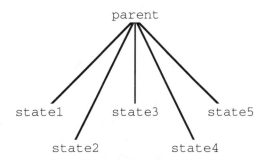

Figure 8.2 Inheritance hierarchy

The base class, `parent`, has an unusual combination of members:

```
struct parent
{
    static char* expression;
    static index;
    static end_state;    // 1 when last state is reached, 0
                         // otherwise
    static doom_state;   // 1 when illegal input occurs, 0
                         // otherwise
    parent( char* expr );
    virtual parent* transition() {}
};

parent::parent( char* expr )
{
    expression = new char[ strlen( expr ) ];
    strcpy( expression, expr );
    end_state = 0;
    doom_state = 0;
    index = 0;
}
```

All the data members of `parent` are static, which suggests that `parent` is a module, like the `HeapStats` module seen in Chapter 7. A class module is not instantiated to create objects; instead, its static data members record the module's state. However, `parent` has a constructor, which suggests that the class will be instantiated, since constructors execute only when objects are created. This constructor assigns what appear to be initial values to the static data members, although they must have been previously initialized elsewhere. There is also a virtual function, `transition()`, which should return a pointer but lacks a `return` statement in its body, which suggests that `parent` should be an abstract base class. (Not all compilers flag the missing return as the error it is.) The declaration of `parent` delivers mixed signals about the role of this class, making it difficult to understand the program.

When faced with a new program, it is usually best to examine class interfaces and inheritance relationships to understand the architecture in-the-large before worrying about the details. That has been our approach in the little distance we have come with this program, and we might now continue by inspecting the inheritance relationships. However, this program's unorthodox architecture makes it difficult to attack conventionally. We will therefore take a completely different approach and trace its control flow to uncover the design in a bottom-up fashion.

The trace must start before `main()`, with the execution of the constructors for the global objects s1 through s5. The first object initialized is s1. Its type is state1, which has two constructors, base and derived. The derived constructor has an empty body, but passes an argument to the base constructor:

```
struct state1 : public parent
{
    parent *ptr2, *ptr3, *ptr4, *ptr5;
    state1() : parent( expression ) {}
    parent* transition();
};
```

The argument to the base constructor, `expression`, is a static member of `parent`, and its initial value is a null pointer. So `parent::parent()`, executing for s1, receives a null pointer as its argument:

```
parent::parent( char* expr )
{
    expression = new char[ strlen( expr ) ];
    strcpy( expression, expr );
    end_state = 0;
    doom_state = 0;
    index = 0;
}
```

Look at the null argument to `parent::parent()`; clearly, something is wrong: `expression` itself, currently a null pointer, is the argument string that `parent::parent()` duplicates and saves back in `expression`. There is no guarantee about what `strlen()` will do with a null pointer; it depends on the implementation. On the one hand, `strlen()` may immediately fault on indirection through the null pointer. On the other hand, the null pointer may address readable memory, in which case `strlen()` finds the length of the string starting at that address (assuming a terminating null byte is found). If `strlen()` does return, another (minor) problem arises immediately: The length returned by `strlen()` does not include the null byte, so the size of the dynamically allocated character array is one less than needed. This off-by-one error is a common problem in C programs and can happen just as easily when manipulating character arrays in C++.

▶ **Remember the null byte — use**
new char[strlen(s)+1].

The off-by-one error need not be fatal. If the size of the block allocated from the heap has to be rounded up for alignment, there will be extra space for `strcpy()` to store a null byte. Such implementation idiosyncrasies permitting, `expression` becomes a pointer to a copy of whatever string is addressed by the null pointer. Surely, this cannot have been the programmer's intention. Let's continue the trace and discover the source of the trouble.

The constructor for `s2` executes next. Again `expression` is the argument to the base constructor, and `expression` is made to point to yet another copy of the string addressed by the null pointer. (Among the least of our concerns, the first copy becomes garbage memory, because no pointer remains with which to delete it.) The constructors for `s3` through `s5` follow, each making a fresh copy of the string.

Once the construction of the global objects is complete, `main()` executes and immediately calls `build_state_machine()`:

```
void build_state_machine()
{
    s1.ptr2 = &s2;
    s1.ptr3 = &s3;
    s1.ptr4 = &s4;
    s1.ptr5 = &s5;
    s2.ptr2 = &s2;
    s3.ptr3 = &s3;
    s3.ptr4 = &s4;
    s4.ptr4 = &s4;
    s5.ptr2 = &s2;
    s5.ptr4 = &s4;
    s5.ptr5 = &s5;
}
```

The regularity of the function body is revealing. Every statement has the same form: `sj.ptri = &si`. Every `ptri` in every `sj` points to the global `si`. Looking through the rest of the program, we see that these pointers never change. So any use of `ptri` in any `sj::transition()` function can be replaced by `&si`. The contribution from `build_state_machine()` is negligible; it has added nothing that was not already present in another form. The `ptri` members of each state structure can be eliminated, with each use of `ptri` replaced by `&si`. After this elimination, `state1::transition`, for example, would become

```
parent* state1::transition()
{
    switch( expression[ index++ ] )
    {
        case 'A':
            return &s2;
        case 'B':
            return &s3;
        case 'C':
            return &s4;
        case 'D':
            return &s5;
        case '\0':
            doom_state = 1;
        default:
            doom_state = 1;
    }
}
```

If the pointers are eliminated from the state structures, and each pointer re-placed by the corresponding address in the `transition()` functions, `build_state_machine()` is redundant.

If `build_state_machine()` is eliminated, then `main()` starts by prompting for, and gathering, an input string:

```
char input_string[80];
printf("Enter input expression: ");
scanf("%s", input_string);
parent state_machine(input_string);
```

The input string becomes a parameter to the constructor of a `parent` object in a dec-laration that reveals a great deal about the program as a whole. This declaration will soon explain the strange constructors encountered earlier. An automatic instance of `parent` is created. The constructor saves, in `parent::expression`, a pointer to a copy of `input_string`. Finally, we see the purpose of the constructor — to enable a client to transmit to the FSM module a string to be scanned. The question is: Why use a constructor? Indeed, why create an instance of `parent` in `main()`? The auto-matic object `state_machine` is not used again (fortunately, since its `transition()` member function returns no result). The declaration of `state_machine` exists only for the side effect of executing its constructor.

The `parent` constructor sets the state of the FSM module, that is, the static members, in preparation for scanning a string. Almost all of the state of the FSM is recorded in the static members of `parent`, namely, `expression`, `index`, `end_state` and `doom_state`. The one exception is the current state (1 through 5) of the FSM, which is recorded by the variable `ptr` in `main()`. We examine this discrepancy later. Primarily, the constructor puts the FSM into its initial state, ready to scan a string. Now, the purpose of constructors is initialization. So what has gone wrong?

The problem results from two different interpretations of the word *initialization*. Resetting an FSM to its start state is not initialization in the sense of a C++ constructor. The FSM module is a set of static variables whose lifetimes all started at the beginning of the program's execution, when their C++ initialization occurred. Resetting the FSM to its start state, by assigning values to the static members, is an operation on the module, which should be implemented by a static member function. A C++ constructor performs a specific kind of initialization, establishing the initial value of an object at the beginning of its lifetime. The object, `state_machine`, for which the constructor executes, has no non-static members and needs no initialization.

▶ **Don't use a constructor to initialize static data members.**

The root of this program's problems is an attempt to use a constructor for something other than initializing an object. The problems compound because the spurious constructor in the base class demands an argument from an initializer in the constructor defined for each derived class. The derived constructors were probably added to placate a compiler that (quite rightly) complained about missing initializers. The derived constructors then caused the irrelevant and erroneous construction of `s1` through `s5`. The derived constructors have no true purpose and should be eliminated.

Six steps are needed to correct the problems encountered thus far. Listing 8.2 shows the result of taking the following six steps:

1. Replace the `parent` constructor by a static member function called, say, `reset()`.

2. Correct the off-by-one error.

3. Remove `state_machine` from `main()` and call `parent::reset()` directly instead.

4. Remove the constructor from each `state`*j*.

5. Remove the `state`*j*`::ptr`*i* members and use `&s`*i* in the `transition()` functions instead.

6. Remove `build_state_machine()`.

Listing 8.2 `parent::parent()` replaced by `reset()`

```
#include <string.h>

struct parent
{
    static char *expression;
    static index;
    static end_state;   // 1 when last state is reached, 0
                        // otherwise
    static doom_state;  // 1 when illegal input occurs, 0
                        // otherwise
    static void reset( char* expr );
    virtual parent* transition() {}
};

void parent::reset( char* expr )
{
    expression = new char[ strlen( expr ) + 1 ];
    strcpy( expression, expr );
    end_state = 0;
    doom_state = 0;
    index = 0;
}

struct state1 : public parent
{
    parent* transition();
};

// ...

struct state5 : public parent
{
    parent* transition();
};

char* parent::expression = NULL;
int parent::doom_state = 0;
int parent::end_state = 0;
int parent::index = 0;

state1 s1;
state2 s2;
state3 s3;
state4 s4;
state5 s5;
```

```cpp
parent* state1::transition()
{
    switch( expression[ index++ ] )
    {
        case 'A':
            return &s2;
        case 'B':
            return &s3;
        case 'C':
            return &s4;
        case 'D':
            return &s5;
        case '\0':
            doom_state = 1;
        default:
            doom_state = 1;
    }
}

// ...

parent* state5::transition()
{
    switch( expression[ index++ ] )
    {
        case 'O':
            return &s2;
        case 'H':
            return &s5;
        case 'L':
            end_state = 1;
            break;
        case 'N':
            return &s4;
        case '\0':
            doom_state = 1;
        default:
            doom_state = 1;
    }
}

#include <stdio.h>
```

```
main()
{
    char input_string[80];
    printf("Enter input expression: ");
    scanf("%s", input_string);
    parent::reset(input_string);
    parent* ptr;
    ptr = s1.transition();
    while( ptr->end_state != 1 && ptr->doom_state != 1 )
    {
        ptr = ptr->transition();
    }
    if( ptr->end_state == 1 )
        printf("\nValid input expression");
    else
        printf("\nInvalid input expression");
    return 0;
}
```

Coupling

In Listing 8.2, main() no longer declares a parent object. The FSM is reset by parent::reset(), called from main(). With the FSM reset, main() loops, making transitions on the FSM:

```
    parent::reset(input_string);
    parent* ptr;
    ptr = s1.transition();
    while( ptr->end_state != 1 && ptr->doom_state != 1 )
    {
        ptr = ptr->transition();
    }
```

It is the ptr variable in main() that records the current state of the FSM, getting its first value from the transition out of the start state. We see from the loop that the coupling between main() and parent is high — they depend intimately on one another, with responsibilities distributed between them. The most crucial part of the FSM, its current state, is stored in a variable in main(), while the FSM manages the source of characters that drive it. An FSM should be concerned with how to react to each input character, not how to manage character strings. Responsibilities are distributed between main() and parent such that each is doing some of the other's job. To reduce the coupling, the character string should be isolated within main(), and the current state of the FSM should be isolated within parent.

▶ **Reduce coupling — minimize interactions between classes.**

To reduce coupling, `parent::expression` and the argument to `reset()` should be eliminated, and the index in `parent::index` should become a local variable in `main()`. To obtain the current input, `transition()` must take a character argument, which `main()` supplies.

The variable that carries the current state of the FSM must move from `main()` into `parent` and should receive a more meaningful name than `ptr`. Let `current` be a static member of `parent` that points to the current state:

```
struct parent
{
    static parent* current; // &s1 .. &s5
    // ...
```

What value should `current` have when the FSM is in the doom state or end state? There is a simple way for `current` itself to represent all the information that was originally in the flags `end_state` and `doom_state`. In the transition graph, state 6 represented the end state. We can introduce `s6` and represent the end state by having `current` point to `s6`. In the doom state there is no state, represented naturally by the null pointer. The static members `end_state` and `doom_state` become redundant.

```
struct parent
{
    static parent* current; // &s1 .. &s6; NULL => doom
    // ...
};

// ...

parent* state2::transition(char x)
{
    switch( x )
    {
        case 'E':
            return &s2;
        case 'I':
            return &s6;
        default:
            return NULL;
    }
}
```

Notice that the transition functions now always execute a `return` statement. The original versions (in Listing 8.1) did not return a pointer when `doom_state` or `end_state` was true, causing `ptr` in `main()` to become undefined. The program survived the undefined pointer because indirection through the `ptr` in `main()` accessed only static members of `parent`, an operation independent of the pointer's value (see Ellis and Stroustrup, page 180). It is shortsighted to allow an undefined return value from a function just because a particular client does not depend on it. The transition functions now always return a well-defined value.

We can improve the encapsulation of `parent` by making `current` a private member, hiding the representation of the state of the FSM from the remainder of the program. The public interface to the `parent` module is then a set of static member functions that manipulate and interrogate the state of the FSM:

```
class parent
{
    static parent *current;      // &s1 .. &s6; NULL => doom
protected:
    virtual parent* transition(char) {}
public:
    static void reset();         // move to start state
    static void advance(char);   // advance one transition
    static int  end_state();
    static int  doom_state();
};
```

Since `current` is now private and `transition()` is invoked with respect to the current state, it no longer makes sense for `main()` to call `transition()` directly. A new public member function, `advance()`, lets `main()` drive the FSM to its next state. The derived `state`*j* classes must still be able to override `transition()`, so access to `transition()` should be protected. For determining the condition of the FSM, the functions `doom_state()` and `end_state()`, which test `current`, replace their namesakes.

The net change to the program from the version in Listing 8.2 is the decoupling of `parent` and `main()` and the better encapsulation of `parent`. The string to be scanned is exclusively in `main()`; the state of the FSM is exclusively in `parent`. Study Listing 8.3 to see the program's new organization, and consider what further improvements might be made.

Listing 8.3 `parent` and `main()` decoupled

```
#include <string.h>

class parent
{
    static parent *current;      // &s1 .. &s6; NULL => doom
protected:
    virtual parent* transition(char) {}
public:
    static void reset();         // move to start state
    static void advance(char);   // advance one transition
    static int   end_state();
    static int   doom_state();
};

struct state1 : public parent
{
    parent* transition(char);
};

// ...

struct state6 : public parent
{
    parent* transition(char);
};

parent* parent::current = NULL;

state1 s1;
state2 s2;
state3 s3;
state4 s4;
state5 s5;
state6 s6;

void parent::reset()
{
    current = &s1;
}

void parent::advance(char x)
{
    if( current )
        current = current->transition(x);
}

int parent::end_state()
{
    return current == &s6;
}
```

```
int parent::doom_state()
{
    return current == NULL;
}

parent* state1::transition(char x)
{
    switch( x )
    {
        case 'A':
            return &s2;
        case 'B':
            return &s3;
        case 'C':
            return &s4;
        case 'D':
            return &s5;
        default:
            return NULL;
    }
}

// ...

parent* state6::transition(char)
{
    return NULL;
}

#include <stdio.h>

main()
{
    char input_string[80];
    printf("Enter input expression: ");
    scanf("%s", input_string);
    parent::reset();
    int index = 0;
    parent::advance(input_string[index++]);
    while( !parent::end_state() && !parent::doom_state() )
    {
        parent::advance(input_string[index++]);
    }
    if( parent::end_state() )
        printf("\nValid input expression");
    else
        printf("\nInvalid input expression");
    return 0;
}
```

Cohesion

We can now examine the inheritance relationship between `parent` and the `state`j structures. The generic identifier `parent` tells us little about the purpose of this class. Its purpose turns out to be twofold. First, it is the module that records the state of the FSM. Second, it serves as an abstract base class for the structures that characterize the individual states. An FSM and its states are related, but not by the specialization, "is a kind of," relationship. Rather, part of an FSM is its set of states. The FSM and state abstractions must be made distinct. Should `parent` be the abstraction of a state of the FSM or the abstraction of an FSM as a whole?

Unfortunately, `parent` is trying to be both a state and the FSM itself. Ideally, a well-designed software component serves only one clearly defined purpose, which forms a coherent thread throughout the component. By serving two purposes at once, `parent` exhibits poor cohesion. Rather than argue about whether `parent` is really a state or the FSM as a whole, it is simpler to recognize the two distinct abstractions and divide `parent` into two distinct classes: `state` and `fsm`. The `state` structure is exclusively the abstract base class for the states; the `fsm` class is exclusively the FSM module.

▶ **Each class should serve a single, coherent purpose.**

At last, we have simple, coherent definitions of state and FSM:

```
struct state
{
    virtual state* transition(char) = 0;
};

class fsm
{
    static state* current;      // &s1 .. &s6; NULL => doom
public:
    static void reset();        // move to start state
    static void advance(char);  // advance one transition
    static int  end_state();
    static int  doom_state();
};
```

Note that `state::transition()` is now a pure virtual function, making `state` formally an abstract base class. Listing 8.4 shows the program with `parent` separated into `state` and `fsm`.

Listing 8.4 parent separated in state and fsm

```cpp
#include <string.h>

struct state
{
    virtual state* transition(char) = 0;
};

class fsm
{
    static state* current;      // &s1 .. &s6; NULL => doom
public:
    static void reset();        // move to start state
    static void advance(char);  // advance one transition
    static int  end_state();
    static int  doom_state();
};

struct state1 : public state
{
    state* transition(char);
};

// ...

struct state6 : public state
{
    state* transition(char);
};

state* fsm::current = NULL;

state1 s1;
state2 s2;
state3 s3;
state4 s4;
state5 s5;
state6 s6;

void fsm::reset()
{
    current = &s1;
}

void fsm::advance(char x)
{
    if( current )
        current = current->transition(x);
}
```

```
int fsm::end_state()
{
    return current == &s6;
}

int fsm::doom_state()
{
    return current == NULL;
}

state* state1::transition(char x)
{
    switch( x )
    {
        case 'A':
            return &s2;
        case 'B':
            return &s3;
        case 'C':
            return &s4;
        case 'D':
            return &s5;
        default:
            return NULL;
    }
}

// ...

state* state6::transition(char)
{
    return NULL;
}

#include <stdio.h>
```

```
main()
{
    char input_string[80];
    printf("Enter input expression: ");
    scanf("%s", input_string);
    fsm::reset();
    int index = 0;
    fsm::advance(input_string[index++]);
    while( !fsm::end_state() && !fsm::doom_state() )
    {
        fsm::advance(input_string[index++]);
    }
    if( fsm::end_state() )
        printf("\nValid input expression");
    else
        printf("\nInvalid input expression");
    return 0;
}
```

Modules versus Abstract Data Types

Class `fsm` is still a module, a set of static variables manipulated by a set of static functions. There is rarely a reason to restrict a class to the role of a module if it is equally easy to create an abstract data type (ADT), which can be instantiated as often as needed.

▶ **Design abstract data types rather than modules.**

Here, `fsm` is easily converted from a class module to an ADT by removing `static` from the member declarations and adding a constructor:

```
class fsm
{
    state* current;     // &s1 .. &s6; NULL => doom
public:
    void reset();       // move to start state
    void advance(char); // advance one transition
    int  end_state();
    int  doom_state();
         fsm();
};
```

Ironically, to use `fsm` as an ADT, we must now reintroduce a declaration in `main()` similar to the one discarded in an earlier transformation. An `fsm` object must be created in `main()`:

```
main()
{
    char input_string[80];
    printf("Enter input expression: ");
    scanf("%s", input_string);
    fsm m;
    m.reset();
    int index = 0;
    m.advance(input_string[index++]);
```

In this code, the `fsm` object, `m`, is an intrinsic part of the computation, not an artifact of passing a value to a module. Each `fsm` object — there may now be more than one — stores its own current state. The `fsm` constructor takes no argument; the scanned string stays within the client, in this case `main()`. No longer static, the member functions of `fsm` must be invoked with respect to an `fsm` object, for example, `m.reset()`. See Listing 8.5.

Listing 8.5 `fsm` converted from module to ADT

```
#include <string.h>

struct state
{
    virtual state* transition(char) = 0;
};

class fsm
{
    state* current;      // &s1 .. &s6; NULL => doom
public:
    void reset();        // move to start state
    void advance(char);  // advance one transition
    int  end_state();
    int  doom_state();
         fsm();
};

struct state1 : public state
{
    state* transition(char);
};

// ...

struct state6 : public state
{
    state* transition(char);
};
```

```
state1 s1;
state2 s2;
state3 s3;
state4 s4;
state5 s5;
state6 s6;

fsm::fsm()
{
    current = NULL;
}

void fsm::reset()
{
    current = &s1;
}

void fsm::advance(char x)
{
    if( current )
        current = current->transition(x);
}

int fsm::end_state()
{
    return current == &s6;
}

int fsm::doom_state()
{
    return current == NULL;
}

state* state1::transition(char x)
{
    switch( x )
    {
        case 'A':
            return &s2;
        case 'B':
            return &s3;
        case 'C':
            return &s4;
        case 'D':
            return &s5;
        default:
            return NULL;
    }
}

// ...
```

```
state* state6::transition(char)
{
    return NULL;
}

#include <stdio.h>

main()
{
    char input_string[80];
    printf("Enter input expression: ");
    scanf("%s", input_string);
    fsm m;
    m.reset();
    int index = 0;
    m.advance(input_string[index++]);
    while( !m.end_state() && !m.doom_state() )
    {
        m.advance(input_string[index++]);
    }
    if( m.end_state() )
        printf("\nValid input expression");
    else
        printf("\nInvalid input expression");
    return 0;
}
```

Value versus Behavior

The program in Listing 8.5 is easier to understand and permits evaluation of an important design decision that would have been difficult to isolate in the original code. The essence of the design is now clear:

1. The transition graph characterizes the FSM.

2. Each node in the transition graph corresponds to a state object.

3. Each state object maps any input character to another state object.

This design is sound, as far as it goes. The next step is a decision about how to characterize the states. What do states have in common, and what distinguishes one state from another? What precisely is "stateness"? Ignoring the distinction of the start and end states, the answer is simple: Each state provides a mapping from input characters to successor states. Apart from the value of that mapping, all states are alike in that each performs a mapping. The original source code reflects the uniform behavior of states. There is a single operation on a state, implemented as the `transition()` virtual member function.

The "value" of the mapping characterizes a given state, a value that must have a representation. There are two basic ways to represent a mapping in a computer program: a table or an algorithm, which in terms of a C++ program means either passive data or executable code. When deciding how to implement a given mapping, the choice between data and code is not always easy. Sometimes a hybrid technique is needed because neither works well by itself. In this program, code — the `transition()` functions — represents the mappings. As a consequence, the program is more complicated and less general than it would be if the mappings were represented by data.

Looking at a `transition()` function, we see remarkable regularity in the cases of the `switch` statements; for example:

```
state* state2::transition(char x)
{
    switch( x )
    {
        case 'E':
            return &s2;
        case 'I':
            return &s6;
        default:
            return NULL;
    }
}
```

Each case of the `switch` statement supplies a value. There is no variation in behavior from case to case. The same information could be encoded in a table, eliminating many functions from the program. Each state has a transition table, an array indexed by input characters, that represents its mapping. If a table captures the variation from state to state, there is no need for a different type for each state, nor for inheritance or virtual functions. A single `state` structure is sufficient:

```
#include <limits.h>

const int range = CHAR_MAX+1; // 0 .. CHAR_MAX
```

```
struct state
{
    state*  transition[range];
          state();
};
```

For any state `s` and input character `c` the successor state is given by `s.transition[c]`. A rule from Chapter 1 is applicable:

> ▶ **Use data members for variation in value; reserve virtual functions for variation in behavior.**

The FSM still requires one state object per node in the transition graph. An array of states in `fsm` suffices:

```
class fsm
{
    state  graph[6];     // transition graph; [0] is end state
    state* current;      // &graph[0] .. &graph[5]; NULL => doom
public:
    void reset();        // move to start state
    void advance(char);  // advance one transition
    int  end_state();
    int  doom_state();
         fsm();
};
```

`fsm::graph[]` has six elements for six states, indexed from zero through five. With zero-based indexing in C++, it is natural to place the end state (what was `s6`) at position zero.

The transition array within each state must be initialized to configure the FSM, a task for the `fsm` constructor. A vector of triples, terminated by a sentinel, encodes the transition graph:

```
struct triple {
    int  from;      // current state
    char input;     // input character
    int  to;        // next state
};
```

```
fsm::fsm()
{
    static triple edges[] = {
        {1, 'A', 2}, {1, 'B', 3}, {1, 'C', 4}, {1, 'D', 5},
        {2, 'E', 2}, {2, 'I', 0},
        {3, 'F', 3}, {3, 'J', 0}, {3, 'M', 4},
        {4, 'G', 4}, {4, 'K', 0},
        {5, 'H', 5}, {5, 'L', 0}, {5, 'O', 2}, {5, 'N', 4},
        {0,  0 , 0}
    };

    for( triple* e = edges; e->from != 0; ++e )
        graph[e->from].transition[e->input] = &graph[e->to];
    current = NULL;
}
```

The implementation of f sm has changed radically — virtual functions have been replaced by data tables — without altering two properties of the program. First, the underlying intent in the design remains that an FSM is a set of state objects. Second, the public interface of f sm remains the same, so main() does not change. See Listing 8.6.

Listing 8.6 Transition mappings represented by tables

```
#include <string.h>
#include <limits.h>

const int range = CHAR_MAX+1; // 0  .. CHAR_MAX

struct state
{
    state*  transition[range];
            state();
};

class fsm
{
    state  graph[6];     // transition graph; [0] is end state
    state* current;      // &graph[0] .. &graph[5]; NULL => doom
public:
    void reset();        // move to start state
    void advance(char);  // advance one transition
    int  end_state();
    int  doom_state();
         fsm();
};
```

```
state::state()
{
    for( int i = 0; i < range; ++i )
        transition[i] = NULL;
}

struct triple {
    int   from;        // current state
    char  input;       // input character
    int   to;          // next state
};

fsm::fsm()
{
    static triple edges[] = {
        {1, 'A', 2}, {1, 'B', 3}, {1, 'C', 4}, {1, 'D', 5},
        {2, 'E', 2}, {2, 'I', 0},
        {3, 'F', 3}, {3, 'J', 0}, {3, 'M', 4},
        {4, 'G', 4}, {4, 'K', 0},
        {5, 'H', 5}, {5, 'L', 0}, {5, 'O', 2}, {5, 'N', 4},
        {0,  0 , 0}
    };

    for( triple* e = edges; e->from != 0; ++e )
        graph[e->from].transition[e->input] = &graph[e->to];
    current = NULL;
}

void fsm::reset()
{
    current = &graph[1];
}

void fsm::advance(char x)
{
    if( current )
        current = current->transition[x];
}

int fsm::end_state()
{
    return current == &graph[0];
}

int fsm::doom_state()
{
    return current == NULL;
}

#include <stdio.h>
```

```
main()
{
    char input_string[80];
    printf("Enter input expression: ");
    scanf("%s", input_string);
    fsm m;
    m.reset();
    int index = 0;
    m.advance(input_string[index++]);
    while( !m.end_state() && !m.doom_state() )
    {
        m.advance(input_string[index++]);
    }
    if( m.end_state() )
        printf("\nValid input expression");
    else
        printf("\nInvalid input expression");
    return 0;
}
```

Generalization

A major weakness remains in the program. It is possible to create an arbitrary number of instances of class fsm, but each fsm object must be a copy of the same FSM, with exactly the same behavior. Having defined an FSM abstraction, it makes sense to generalize the class to handle an arbitrary transition graph.

▶ **Don't solve a specific case if the general case is as simple.**

If the class fsm could represent any FSM, it would better deserve its name. The specific configuration performed by the constructor should be generalized to a mechanism that allows any FSM to be built. The fsm constructor, instead of containing a specific transition graph, should take a transition graph as an argument. The argument can be a vector of triples, as above. If the graph is an argument, its size can no longer be hard-coded in fsm, but must be determined by the constructor. The constructor must dynamically create an array of states, and a destructor must be added to destroy the array:

```
class fsm
{
    state* graph;       // transition graph; [0] is end state
    state* current;     // &graph[0] .. &graph[N-1]; NULL => doom
public:
    void reset();       // move to start state
    void advance(char); // advance one transition
    int  end_state();
    int  doom_state();
         fsm(triple*);
virtual  ~fsm();
};

fsm::fsm(triple* p)
{
    int max_node = 0;    // size for dynamically allocated graph
    for( triple* e = p; e->from; ++e ){
        if( e->from > max_node )
            max_node = e->from;
        if( e->to > max_node )
            max_node = e->to;
    }
    graph = new state[max_node+1];
    for( e = p ; e->from; ++e )
        graph[e->from].transition[e->input] = &graph[e->to];
    current = NULL;
}

fsm::~fsm()
{
    delete [] graph;
}
```

The `fsm` class is now more flexible. Anywhere an `fsm` object is created, an array describing an appropriate transition graph is supplied. The disadvantage to this flexibility is that every creator of an FSM is obliged to provide a transition graph. A program in which all FSMs are based on the same transition graph does not exploit the flexibility, and the extra effort to create an FSM becomes a burden. Classes that specialize `fsm` by binding a specific transition graph into their definition can simplify declarations in such programs. Inheritance from `fsm` as a base class permits the specialization. The derived constructor provides the transition graph:

```
class sample : public fsm
{
    static triple edges[];
public:
    sample();
};
```

```
triple sample::edges[] = {
    {1, 'A', 2}, {1, 'B', 3}, {1, 'C', 4}, {1, 'D', 5},
    {2, 'E', 2}, {2, 'I', 0},
    {3, 'F', 3}, {3, 'J', 0}, {3, 'M', 4},
    {4, 'G', 4}, {4, 'K', 0},
    {5, 'H', 5}, {5, 'L', 0}, {5, 'O', 2}, {5, 'N', 4},
    {0,  0 , 0}
};

sample::sample() : fsm(edges)
{
}
```

Class `sample` extends class `fsm`, but only with respect to initialization. Once constructed, a `sample` object is manipulated as an `fsm` object through its inherited member functions. After construction, the behavior of a `sample` object is indistinguishable from that of an `fsm` object based on the same transition graph.

As discussed in Chapter 4, since fsm is now a base class, its destructor should be virtual. Class `sample` does not define a destructor, but other derived classes may.

> ▶ **Usually, the destructor in a public base class should be**
> **virtual.**

Clients instantiate `sample`, ignorant of how the derived constructor performs the base initialization. For example, the beginning of `main()` becomes

```
main()
{
    char input_string[80];
    printf("Enter input expression: ");
    scanf("%s", input_string);
    sample m;
    m.reset();
```

Listing 8.7 shows the final version of the whole program.

Listing 8.7 `sample` specializes `fsm`

```
#include <string.h>
#include <limits.h>

const int range = CHAR_MAX+1; // 0 .. CHAR_MAX
```

```
struct state
{
    state*  transition[range];
            state();
};

struct triple {
    int  from;        // current state
    char input;       // input character
    int  to;          // next state
};

class fsm
{
    state* graph;         // transition graph; [0] is end state
    state* current;       // &graph[0] .. &graph[N-1]; NULL => doom
public:
    void reset();         // move to start state
    void advance(char);   // advance one transition
    int  end_state();
    int  doom_state();
         fsm(triple*);
virtual  ~fsm();
};

state::state()
{
    for( int i = 0; i < range; ++i )
        transition[i] = NULL;
}

fsm::fsm(triple* p)
{
    int max_node = 0;     // size for dynamically allocated graph
    for( triple* e = p; e->from; ++e ){
        if( e->from > max_node )
            max_node = e->from;
        if( e->to > max_node )
            max_node = e->to;
    }
    graph = new state[max_node+1];
    for( e = p ; e->from; ++e )
        graph[e->from].transition[e->input] = &graph[e->to];
    current = NULL;
}

fsm::~fsm()
{
    delete [] graph;
}
```

```
void fsm::reset()
{
    current = &graph[1];
}

void fsm::advance(char x)
{
    if( current )
        current = current->transition[x];
}

int fsm::end_state()
{
    return current == &graph[0];
}

int fsm::doom_state()
{
    return current == NULL;
}

class sample : public fsm
{
    static triple edges[];
public:
    sample();
};

triple sample::edges[] = {
    {1, 'A', 2}, {1, 'B', 3}, {1, 'C', 4}, {1, 'D', 5},
    {2, 'E', 2}, {2, 'I', 0},
    {3, 'F', 3}, {3, 'J', 0}, {3, 'M', 4},
    {4, 'G', 4}, {4, 'K', 0},
    {5, 'H', 5}, {5, 'L', 0}, {5, 'O', 2}, {5, 'N', 4},
    {0,  0 , 0}
};

sample::sample() : fsm(edges)
{
}

#include <stdio.h>
```

```
main()
{
    char input_string[80];
    printf("Enter input expression: ");
    scanf("%s", input_string);
    sample m;
    m.reset();
    int index = 0;
    m.advance(input_string[index++]);
    while( !m.end_state() && !m.doom_state() )
    {
        m.advance(input_string[index++]);
    }
    if( m.end_state() )
        printf("\nValid input expression");
    else
        printf("\nInvalid input expression");
    return 0;
}
```

Bibliographic Notes

Finite state machines, also known as finite automata, are formally described in many texts on compilers, formal languages and discrete mathematics. For examples, see Hopcroft and Ullman [2].

1. Ellis, M. A., and Stroustrup, B. 1990. *The Annotated C++ Reference Manual.* Reading, MA: Addison-Wesley.

2. Hopcroft, J. E. and Ullman, J. D. 1969. *Formal Languages and their Relation to Automata.* Reading, MA: Addison-Wesley.

Exercises

8.1. What would be required to convert class `fsm` of Listing 8.7 into a conventional FSM? A conventional FSM does not have a special "end state." Rather, any subset of its states is designated as the "accepting" states. At any time the machine can perform a transition or indicate whether or not it is in an accepting state.

8.2. A typical `transition` array in `state` is likely to be *sparse,* that is, most of the entries are null pointers. How can memory requirements be reduced by changing the representation of a state? What parts of the program must be changed?

9

Multiple Inheritance

Multiple inheritance is a complicated and poorly understood part of C++. At first sight, multiple inheritance is appealing because programmers expect to be able to model multiple "is-a" relationships between natural classes, such as a houseboat is a boat and a houseboat is a house. On closer inspection, multiple inheritance turns out to be difficult to use effectively. The difficulty stems in part from the many subtle interactions hidden in the language semantics; it is hard to make programs behave as intended. The difficulty is also due to the limited situations in which the multiple inheritance mechanism supports useful relationships. This chapter studies the semantics of multiple inheritance, examines two situations in which multiple inheritance fails, and then shows one example of multiple inheritance solving a problem.

Ambiguities under Multiple Inheritance

Before looking at programs that use multiple inheritance, we should study some of its complexities. On most language topics the reader's knowledge of C++ has been assumed, and only a few language details have been clarified. Some parts of multiple inheritance are sufficiently subtle that they warrant explicit explanation. A programmer considering using multiple inheritance must look beyond the basic language mechanism and understand its subtleties before proceeding. The treatment given here is by no means exhaustive, but offers some guidance on which parts of multiple inheritance deserve detailed study before use.

The complexities of multiple inheritance stem from numerous kinds of ambiguities that can arise. The simplest form of ambiguity under multiple inheritance is a name conflict among the members of multiple base classes. Consider class `Derived` in Listing 9.1. Both base classes, `Base1` and `Base2`, define a member function called `f`.

Listing 9.1 Ambiguous base member function

```
class Base1 {
    // ...
public:
    void f();
    void g();
    // ...
};

class Base2 {
    // ...
public:
    void f();
    void h();
    // ...
};

class Derived : public Base1, public Base2 {
    // ...
};
```

The base member functions `Base1::g()` and `Base2::h()` are unambiguous. When called with respect to a `Derived` object, there is only one possible interpretation of which function is meant:

```
    Derived d;
    d.g();          // unambiguous
    d.h();          // unambiguous
```

In contrast, `d.f()` is an ambiguous call. Attempting to call `f()` with respect to a `Derived` object leads to a compile-time ambiguity error:

```
    d.f();          // compile-time error
```

The call could mean either `Base1::f()` or `Base2::f()`. Both `f()` functions are inherited by `Derived` and can execute on behalf of a `Derived` object. This kind of ambiguity may be resolved by using the scope resolution operator to build a fully qualified name in the expression that calls one of the base member functions explicitly:

```
d.Base1::f();    // ambiguity resolved
d.Base2::f();    // ambiguity resolved
```

The ambiguity in the classes shown in Listing 9.1 arises because the functions have the same name, regardless of whether or not they are public member functions. The same ambiguity would occur between a private member of one base class and a public member of another. Access control, that is, public versus private access of members, does not influence the way the scope rules direct the search for the declaration of an identifier. In Listing 9.2, the function `f()` has become a private member of `Base2`. The expression `d.f()` remains ambiguous. Only when scope resolution has been applied so that the function is identified unambiguously does the question of access control arise. Identified by its fully qualified name, `d.Base1::f()` is a public member function, which may be called. On the other hand, `d.Base2::f()` is a private function, which may not be called.

Listing 9.2 Access control does not resolve ambiguity

```
class Base1 {
    // ...
public:
    void f();
    // ...
};

class Base2 {
    void f();
    // ...
public:
    // ...
};

class Derived : public Base1, public Base2 {
    // ...
};
```

```
int main()
{
    Derived d;
    d.f();          // compile-time error: ambiguous f
    // ...
}
```

Directed Acyclic Inheritance Graphs

Further ambiguity arises when a derived class is connected to a base class by more than one path through the inheritance hierarchy. This phenomenon is possible because multiple base classes may in turn have a common base class. A simple way to create multiple paths in an inheritance hierarchy uses four classes, as shown in Listing 9.3. The inheritance relationships between the four classes in Listing 9.3 are shown in Figure 9.1. Note that classes Left and Right have the same common base class and the same common derived class. Under single inheritance, an inheritance hierarchy can always be described by a tree of classes. Under multiple inheritance, a richer structure, a *directed acyclic graph*, is needed. "Directed" means that each edge in the graph has an orientation that distinguishes which end is the base class and which end is the derived class. The convention used throughout this book is that the base class appears above the derived class. "Acyclic" means that the inheritance graph has no loops, or cycles, so a class can never be its own base class, even indirectly.

Listing 9.3 A common base class

```
class Top {
    int x;
    // ...
};

class Left : public Top {
    int y;
    // ...
};

class Right : public Top {
    int z;
    // ...
};

class Bottom : public Left, public Right {
    // ...
};
```

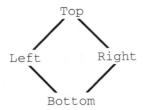

Figure 9.1 A common base class

The configuration of classes in Listing 9.3 deserves close study. In general, every object of any derived class incorporates all the members of every base class. Collectively, the members of a base class within a derived object are called a *base part*. Consider a Bottom object. A Bottom object must contain both a Left base part and a Right base part. In turn, both Left and Right objects contain a Top part. Because the Top part can be reached in two different ways from Bottom, a potential for ambiguity arises. Does a Bottom object contain two Top parts or just one? A Bottom object contains two Top parts if it contains one independently in both its Left part and its Right part. If the Top parts are shared, then a Bottom object contains only one Top part. For the classes shown in Listing 9.3, the answer is that a Bottom object contains two Top parts. The default inheritance mechanism maintains separate copies of the data members inherited from all base classes. The conceptual layout in memory of a Bottom object corresponding to Listing 9.3 is shown in Figure 9.2.

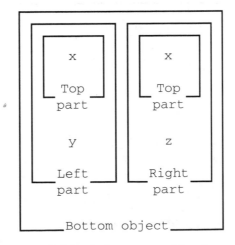

Figure 9.2 Default Bottom object layout

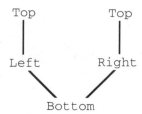

Figure 9.3 Object layout in inheritance hierarchy

To better reflect the fact there are two Top parts in each Bottom object, the inheritance hierarchy may be redrawn to show two appearances of class Top, as in Figure 9.3. This graphical notation combines information about inheritance relationships between classes with information about how inherited state is incorporated into derived objects.

If Top is made into a *virtual base class* of both Left and Right, the number of Top parts in a Bottom object changes. A virtual base class contributes a unique base part to each derived object, regardless of the number of paths by which the virtual base class may be reached. Syntactically, a virtual base class is specified by adding the keyword virtual before the base class name in the derived class declaration. There is no connection between the virtual keyword used in this context and its familiar use in a member function prototype. To make Top a virtual base class, the declarations of Left and Right must be modified, as shown in Listing 9.4.

Listing 9.4 Top as a virtual base class

```
class Top {
    int x;
    // ...
};

class Left : public virtual Top {
    int y;
    // ...
};

class Right : public virtual Top {
    int z;
    // ...
};

class Bottom : public Left, public Right {
    // ...
};
```

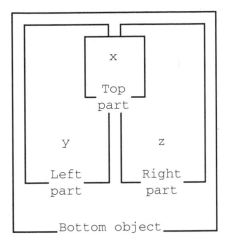

Figure 9.4 `Bottom` object layout with virtual base `Top`

With `Top` as a virtual base class of both `Left` and `Right`, a `Bottom` object contains just one `Top` part, as shown conceptually in Figure 9.4. To indicate the shared base part in a derived object, the inheritance hierarchy as depicted in Figure 9.1 can be reserved for use only when `Top` is a virtual base class.

Virtual base classes are inherently ambiguous. In general, the members of virtual base classes can be named by multiple paths through the inheritance graph. For example, the `x` in a `Bottom` object `b` can be referred to as `b.x`, `b.Left::x`, `b.Right::x`, or `b.Top::x`. For some purposes the multiple paths matter little; for other purposes the programmer must take care to avoid anomalous effects, such as those described below.

Exploring Virtual Base Classes

Let us investigate the behavior of classes `Top`, `Left`, `Right` and `Bottom`, initially with `Top` as a non-virtual base class, and then with `Top` as a virtual base class. Suppose that we define `operator=` for classes `Top`, `Left` and `Right`. As they stand, these classes are not complicated enough to need their own `operator=`, but they will serve to demonstrate the language issues involved. Listing 9.5 shows `Top` as a non-virtual base class and `operator=` defined for all classes except `Bottom`.

Listing 9.5 Assignment with a non-virtual base class

```
void trace(const char *funcName, void *objAddr)
{
    cout << "\t" << objAddr << " " << funcName << "\n";
}

class Top {
    int x;
public:
    Top & operator=(const Top &);
};

Top & Top::operator=(const Top & rhs)
{
    trace("Top::operator=", this);
    if( this != &rhs )
        x = rhs.x;
    return *this;
}

class Left : public Top {
    int y;
public:
    Left & operator=(const Left &);
};

Left & Left::operator=(const Left & rhs)
{
    trace("Left::operator=", this);
    if( this != &rhs ){
        this->Top::operator=(rhs);
        y = rhs.y;
    }
    return *this;
}

class Right : public Top {
    int z;
public:
    Right & operator=(const Right &);
};

Right & Right::operator=(const Right & rhs)
{
    trace("Right::operator=", this);
    if( this != &rhs ){
        this->Top::operator=(rhs);
        z = rhs.z;
    }
    return *this;
}
```

```
class Bottom : public Left, public Right {
    // ...
};

int main()
{
    Left L1, L2;
    Right R1, R2;
    Bottom B1, B2;

    cout << "Left object assignment\n";
    L1 = L2;
    cout << "Right object assignment\n";
    R1 = R2;
    cout << "Bottom object assignment\n";
    B1 = B2;

    return 0;
}
```

The `main()` function in Listing 9.5 performs three assignments. In each assignment, both sides of the assignment are the same type of object: `Left`, `Right` and `Bottom`, respectively. To trace their activity during the assignments, each `operator=` calls `trace()` to display a message identifying the member function and the object for which it is executing. Objects are identified by the value of their `this` pointer. Note that the `this` pointer is converted to a pointer-to-`void` as an argument to `trace()`, after which `cout` converts the pointer-to-`void` to a platform-dependent format, hexadecimal in this case. The output from the program in Listing 9.5 is

```
Left object assignment
    0x72265e Left::operator=
    0x72265e Top::operator=
Right object assignment
    0x72266e Right::operator=
    0x72266e Top::operator=
Bottom object assignment
    0x72267e Left::operator=
    0x72267e Top::operator=
    0x722686 Right::operator=
    0x722686 Top::operator=
```

For assignment of both `Left` and `Right` objects, `Top::operator=` is called to assign the `Top` part of the derived object. For the assignment of a `Bottom` object, class `Bottom` does not declare its own `operator=`, so the compiler supplies `Bottom::operator=` implicitly. The compiler-generated `Bottom::operator=` calls `Left::operator=` and `Right::operator=` in turn to assign the `Left` and

`Right` parts of the `Bottom` object, respectively. We see four assignment operators traced in the output, corresponding to the four parts in Figure 9.2. All is in order. But what happens if `Top` becomes a virtual base class? Listing 9.6 shows `Top` as a virtual base class of `Left` and `Right`.

Listing 9.6 `Top` as a virtual base class

```
class Left : public virtual Top {
    int y;
public:
    Left & operator=(const Left &);
};

class Right : public virtual Top {
    int z;
public:
    Right & operator=(const Right &);
};
```

Assuming the rest of the code from Listing 9.5 remains unaltered, the output from the program in Listing 9.6 is

```
Left object assignment
    0x722642 Left::operator=
    0x72264a Top::operator=
Right object assignment
    0x72265a Right::operator=
    0x722662 Top::operator=
Bottom object assignment
    0x722672 Left::operator=
    0x722682 Top::operator=
    0x72267a Right::operator=
    0x722682 Top::operator=
```

`Top` is now a virtual base class, and each `Bottom` object contains only one `Top` part, as shown in Figure 9.4. However, the output shows `Top::operator=` executing *twice* for the assignment of a `Bottom` object. The addresses in the trace show that `Top::operator=` is executing twice for the same `Top` part. The repeated assignment of the `Top` part is explained by considering each step in the execution of the assignment of a `Bottom` object. The compiler-generated `Bottom::operator=` still calls `operator=` for both its `Left` and `Right` parts, and each in turn still calls `Top::operator=`. Both the `Left` and `Right` parts assume the responsibility for assigning the `Top` part, and therefore it happens twice.

How can the repeated assignment be corrected? The operator= for both Left and Right must call Top::operator=, so that assignment works correctly for Left and Right objects, respectively. A solution is to add another assignment member function to classes Left and Right. The new member function is not an operator function and performs only the local work of assigning the members declared within the class itself. The new member function does not call operator= for the virtual base class. Let this new member function be called assignLocal. With assignLocal in Left and Right, Bottom::operator= can be introduced to provide correct assignment behavior for Bottom objects. Bottom::operator= calls Top::operator= once for the shared Top part and assignLocal for both the Left and Right parts, as shown in Listing 9.7.

Listing 9.7 Virtual base assignment

```
void trace(const char *funcName, void *objAddr)
{
    cout << "\t" << objAddr << " " << funcName << "\n";
}

class Top {
    int x;
public:
    Top & operator=(const Top &);
};

Top & Top::operator=(const Top & rhs)
{
    trace("Top::operator=", this);
    if( this != &rhs )
        x = rhs.x;
    return *this;
}

class Left : public virtual Top {
    int y;
protected:
    void assignLocal(const Left &);
public:
    Left & operator=(const Left &);
};

void Left::assignLocal(const Left & rhs)
{
    trace("Left::assignLocal", this);
    y = rhs.y;
}
```

```
Left & Left::operator=(const Left & rhs)
{
    trace("Left::operator=", this);
    if( this != &rhs ){
        this->Top::operator=(rhs);
        assignLocal(rhs);
    }
    return *this;
}

class Right : public virtual Top {
    int z;
protected:
    void assignLocal(const Right &);
public:
    Right & operator=(const Right &);
};

void Right::assignLocal(const Right & rhs)
{
    trace("Right::assignLocal", this);
    z = rhs.z;
}

Right & Right::operator=(const Right & rhs)
{
    trace("Right::operator=", this);
    if( this != &rhs ){
        this->Top::operator=(rhs);
        assignLocal(rhs);
    }
    return *this;
}

class Bottom : public Left, public Right {
    // ...
public:
    Bottom & operator=(const Bottom &);
};

Bottom & Bottom::operator=(const Bottom & rhs)
{
    trace("Bottom::operator=", this);
    if( this != &rhs ){
        Top::operator=(rhs);
        Left::assignLocal(rhs);
        Right::assignLocal(rhs);
    }
    return *this;
}
```

```
int main()
{
    Left L1, L2;
    Right R1, R2;
    Bottom B1, B2;

    cout << "Left object assignment\n";
    L1 = L2;
    cout << "Right object assignment\n";
    R1 = R2;
    cout << "Bottom object assignment\n";
    B1 = B2;

    return 0;
}
```

The output from the program in Listing 9.7 is

```
Left object assignment
    0x722642 Left::operator=
    0x72264a Top::operator=
    0x722642 Left::assignLocal
Right object assignment
    0x72265a Right::operator=
    0x722662 Top::operator=
    0x72265a Right::assignLocal
Bottom object assignment
    0x722672 Bottom::operator=
    0x722682 Top::operator=
    0x722672 Left::assignLocal
    0x72267a Right::assignLocal
```

Note that `Top::operator=` executes only once in the assignment of a `Bottom` object.

The code in Listing 9.7 is not the only solution to the virtual base assignment problem, but it is simple and symmetric with respect to the intermediate classes, `Left` and `Right`. Nor is Listing 9.7 a complete solution. Class `Bottom` has no `assignLocal()`. If `Bottom` itself serves as a base class to a class that acquires `Top` as a virtual base class by yet another path, the `Top` part would again be assigned more than once. To solve this problem, `Bottom` needs an `assignLocal` that handles the assignment of everything except its virtual base part. In general, an inheritance hierarchy involving virtual base classes must be constructed very carefully to ensure that all objects that can be instantiated from any class in the hierarchy behave consistently. As Ellis and Stroustrup understate on page 296, "Such consistency is not easily achieved for, say, user-defined assignment operators."

This book is not a C++ primer nor reference manual. This sketch of some language details is by no means a comprehensive treatment of multiple inheritance or virtual base classes. The intention here is to convince the reader that there are many subtle details in this part of the language. Before embarking on production programming that uses multiple inheritance and especially virtual base classes, programmers should study the subject carefully.

▶ **Before using virtual base classes, understand them thoroughly.**

An effective way to learn the details of a programming language is to observe how experimental programs behave. Examining the output from a small program and studying how the output changes due to small changes in the program often provide insight into how a programming language works. This technique works for most of C++, but cannot be used reliably for learning multiple inheritance. Unfortunately, virtual base classes are implemented incorrectly by many current C++ compilers, which should not be relied on for learning this part of the language. In preparing the material on virtual base classes, it had been my intention to use a simpler example of virtual base class semantics. I abandoned the simpler example when I discovered that none of my three C++ compilers implemented it correctly. (One compiler crashed, and the other two generated incorrect code — which behavior is preferable?) This example appears as Exercise 9.1.

▶ **Do not try to learn the semantics of multiple inheritance from your compiler.**

The multiple inheritance example code that appears below will not reach the complexity seen above. The remainder of the chapter investigates why multiple inheritance might be needed in writing C++ programs.

Style Example: Class `Monitor`

Listing 9.8 shows class `Monitor` built by multiple inheritance from two base classes, `Dial` and `Sampler`. There is no virtual base class in this example.

Listing 9.8 Classes `Dial`, `Sampler` and `Monitor`

```
class Dial {
    // irrelevant implementation details
  protected:
    double value;
    Dial(char *, double, double);
    ~Dial();
};

class Sampler {
    // implementation details...
    double freq;
  protected:
    virtual void sample();
    Sampler(double);
    ~Sampler();
};

class Monitor : public Dial, public Sampler {
    void sample() { value = get_value(); }
  protected:
    virtual double get_value();
    Monitor(char *lab, double l, double h, double f)
        : Dial(lab, l, h), Sampler(f) {}
};
```

A `Dial` object monitors `Dial::value` and displays the value continuously on a graphics screen. The arguments to the `Dial` constructor are a character string label and a pair of `double` values bounding the range of values that `Dial::value` may assume. A `Sampler` object invokes its `sample()` virtual function every `freq` seconds. The `Sampler` constructor takes a value to initialize `freq`.

The `Monitor` class is derived from both `Dial` and `Sampler`. `Monitor` redefines `Sampler::sample()`, so every `freq` seconds it is `Monitor::sample()` that is called from the `Sampler` part of a `Monitor` object. `Monitor::sample()` in turn calls the virtual function `get_value()` and copies the returned result into `Dial::value`, in the `Dial` part of a `Monitor` object. The `Monitor` constructor merely passes all of its arguments on to the constructors of `Dial` and `Sampler`. To make use of `Monitor`, another class that does define `get_value()` is derived from `Monitor`.

Before addressing the multiple inheritance relationship, the choice of protected access for the members of `Dial` deserves attention. Class `Dial` is constructed in such a way that it can be used *only* by inheritance. Because the constructor is protected, free-standing `Dial` objects may not be instantiated. The following expression is illegal:

```
new Dial("Temp F", 90.0, 110.0);    // compile-time error
```

This restriction on `Dial` is artificial. The `Dial` class is a complete abstraction, and it should be possible to instantiate an object whenever one is required. The constructor and destructor should become public members, as shown in Listing 9.9. Notice that `Dial::value` is also a public member. Public data members are somewhat unusual, but this one serves a precise purpose. The `value` member of `Dial` is part of the class *interface,* not part of the state of a `Dial` object. Other objects communicate with a `Dial` object by writing into `Dial::value`. A `Dial` object receives information by periodically reading the current contents of `value`. The same communication could be achieved by a public member function taking a `double` argument. If `Dial::value` were made private, and a public member function added so that clients could modify value, the client would use different syntax, but `Dial` would not be better encapsulated. Regardless of the interface, `Dial` should be modified so that free-standing objects may be instantiated.

> ► **Avoid artificially limiting a class to serve only as a base class.**

Listing 9.9 The `Dial` interface made public

```
class Dial {
    // irrelevant implementation details
  public:
    double value;
    Dial(char *, double, double);
    virtual ~Dial();
};

class Sampler {
    // implementation details...
    double freq;
  protected:
    virtual void sample() = 0;
    Sampler(double);
    virtual ~Sampler();
};
```

```
class Monitor : public Dial, public Sampler {
    void sample() { value = get_value(); }
  protected:
    virtual double get_value() = 0;
    Monitor(char *lab, double l, double h, double f)
        : Dial(lab, l, h), Sampler(f) {}
};
```

In addition to the `Dial` interface becoming public, there are two other changes between Listing 9.8 and Listing 9.9. First, `Sampler` and `Monitor` have become abstract base classes; each now has a pure virtual function. Neither `Sampler` nor `Monitor` has meaningful implementations of its virtual functions; the classes are not to be instantiated. As abstract base classes, their role in the program is formalized. Second, the `Dial` destructor has been declared virtual. The classes in Listing 9.9 show why the rule about virtual destructors from Chapter 4 is inadequate under multiple inheritance. The rule from Chapter 4 was

> ▶ **If a public base class does not have a virtual destructor,**
> **no derived class nor members of a derived class should**
> **have a destructor.**

Applying this rule, `Monitor` is the derived class, but it has no destructor. Why then must the `Dial` base class destructor be declared virtual? Consider a `Monitor` object deleted through a pointer-to-`Dial`. The destructors for both `Dial` and `Sampler` should execute, not just the `Dial` destructor. A virtual destructor in `Dial` will ensure that all destructors are always called. As the program stands, a virtual destructor is *not* required in `Sampler`. The `Sampler` destructor is protected; thus, a `Monitor` object cannot be deleted through a pointer-to-`Sampler`. A precise rule for exactly when virtual destructors are required under multiple inheritance might be formulated, but a conservative one is simpler to state:

> ▶ **If a multiple inheritance hierarchy has any destructors,**
> **every base class should have a virtual destructor.**

To be cautious, the destructor in `Sampler` has been made virtual.

The Relationship between `Dial` *and* `Monitor`

Why is `Monitor` derived from `Dial`? `Monitor` does not modify nor specialize `Dial`. The interaction between `Monitor` and `Dial` could be expressed in a simpler fashion if `Dial` were a member object of `Monitor`. To see why this is so, suppose `Monitor` had to display both a value and the first derivative of the value. A second `Dial` would be needed for the derivative. A second `Dial` cannot be acquired by multiple inheritance directly from `Dial`, because a class may serve only once as the immediate base of another class. `Monitor` may inherit multiply from `Dial` only if another class is interposed. Suppose that `Dial_1` is derived from `Dial`, but adds no new members. `Dial_1` is then equivalent to `Dial` in terms of behavior, but has a different name. Because it has another name, `Dial_1` may become a third base class of `Monitor`, as shown in Figure 9.5.

A `Monitor` class with multiple `Dial` objects could indeed be built in the manner shown in Figure 9.5, but the style exhibits a syndrome similar to one seen in Chapter 1: Every `Dial` object in `Monitor` requires a separate class declaration. The program in Chapter 1 was improved by identifying better abstractions so that the program had fewer classes. In this program the right abstraction is already present in the `Dial` class. All the `Monitor` class needs to do is instantiate `Dial` objects as members. The simpler way to supply a `Dial` object in a `Monitor` is shown in Listing 9.10.

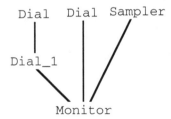

Figure 9.5 A second `Dial` by inheritance

Listing 9.10 `Dial` as a member of `Monitor`

```
class Dial {
    // irrelevant implementation details
  public:
    double value;
    Dial(char *, double, double);
    ~Dial();
};

class Sampler {
    // implementation details...
    double freq;
  protected:
    virtual void sample() = 0;
    Sampler(double);
    virtual ~Sampler();
};

class Monitor : public Sampler {
    Dial display;
    void sample() { display.value = get_value(); }
  protected:
    virtual double get_value() = 0;
    Monitor(char *lab, double l, double h, double f)
        : display(lab, l, h), Sampler(f) {}
};
```

Listing 9.10 shows that the relationship between `Monitor` and `Dial` is that of a client to a server. A `Monitor` object needs the services of a `Dial` object to display a value. For `Dial` and `Monitor`, the lifetime of the server should be the same as the lifetime of its client. Incorporating the server as a base part of the client results in the same lifetime for both objects, but also establishes a gratuitous inheritance relationship. The simpler relationship of the server as a member object of the client is sufficient. This argument is independent of multiple inheritance; in this case it happens to eliminate unnecessary multiple inheritance. The transformation is similar to the elimination of inheritance seen in Chapter 3.

> ▶ **Use a member object, not inheritance, to include a server in a client object.**

Style Example: A Virtual Base Class

In Listing 9.11, class `DomesticAnimal` is a virtual base class. Classes `Cow` and `Buffalo` are derived from `DomesticAnimal`, and class `Beefalo` is derived from both `Cow` and `Buffalo`, as shown in Figure 9.6. Study the classes in Listing 9.11.

Does the multiple inheritance make sense? Is a virtual base class necessary? What simplifications can be made in the code?

Listing 9.11 DomesticAnimal, Cow, Buffalo and Beefalo

```
class DomesticAnimal
{
 protected:
  int weight;
  float price;
  char color[20];
 public:
  DomesticAnimal(void)
   {
    weight = 0;
    price = 0.0;
    strcpy(color, "None");
   }
  DomesticAnimal(int aWeight, float aPrice, char *aColor)
   {
    weight = aWeight;
    price = aPrice;
    strcpy(color, aColor);
   }
  virtual void print(void)
   {
    cout << "The weight = " << weight << "\n";
    cout << "The price = $" << price << "\n";
    cout << "The color = " << color << "\n";
   }
};

class Cow : public virtual DomesticAnimal
{
 public:
  Cow(void)
   {
   }
  Cow(int aWeight, float aPrice, char *aColor)
   {
    weight = aWeight;
    price = aPrice;
    strcpy(color, aColor);
   }
  void print(void)
   {
    cout << "The cow has the properties:\n";
    DomesticAnimal::print();
   }
};
```

```
class Buffalo : public virtual DomesticAnimal
{
 public:
  Buffalo(void)
  {
  }
  Buffalo(int aWeight, float aPrice, char *aColor)
  {
   weight = aWeight;
   price = aPrice;
   strcpy(color, aColor);
  }
  void print(void)
  {
   cout << "The buffalo has the properties:\n";
   DomesticAnimal::print();
  }
};

class Beefalo : public Cow, public Buffalo
{
 public:
  Beefalo(int aWeight, float aPrice, char *aColor)
  {
   weight = aWeight;
   price = aPrice;
   strcpy(color, aColor);
  }
  void print()
  {
   cout << "The beefalo has the properties:\n";
   DomesticAnimal::print();
  }
};

main()
{
 Cow aCow(1400, 375.0, "Black and white");
 Beefalo aBeefalo(1700, 525.0, "Brown and black");

 DomesticAnimal& myCow = aCow;
 DomesticAnimal& myBeefalo = aBeefalo;

 myCow.print();
 myBeefalo.print();
}
```

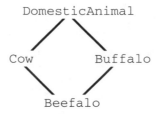

Figure 9.6 DomesticAnimal class hierarchy

The output from the program in Listing 9.11 is

```
The cow has the properties:
The weight = 1400
The price = $375
The color = Black and white
The beefalo has the properties:
The weight = 1700
The price = $525
The color = Brown and black
```

DomesticAnimal makes sense as a base class, because both Cow and Buffalo are specializations of DomesticAnimal. The flawed inheritance relationships are Cow and Buffalo as base classes of Beefalo. The best way to see the flaw is to consider just what Beefalo actually inherits from Cow and Buffalo. For simplicity, we shall examine only the relationship between Beefalo and Cow; the relationship between Beefalo and Buffalo is similar. Cow adds nothing to the interface defined by DomesticAnimal; Cow defines its own print() function and two constructors. Beefalo ignores everything in Cow. Beefalo does not inherit print() from Cow; Beefalo defines its own print(). Beefalo does not communicate through the Cow constructors; indeed, Cow has a default constructor so that Beefalo does not need to mention Cow in an initializer. The Beefalo class almost entirely ignores its immediate base classes. The property of a Beefalo that is acquired from Cow is the legality of a Beefalo object executing Cow::print(). That is, if b is a Beefalo object, then b.Cow::print() is a legal function call, which lets a Beefalo object claim that it is a Cow.

With the exception of making a Beefalo object lie about its identity by explicitly calling a base version of a virtual function, the Beefalo could just as easily be derived directly from DomesticAnimal. The program is rewritten in Listing 9.12, with an inheritance hierarchy as shown in Figure 9.7.

Listing 9.12 Virtual base class eliminated

```cpp
class DomesticAnimal
{
  int weight;
  float price;
  char color[20];
 public:
  DomesticAnimal(void)
  {
   weight = 0;
   price = 0.0;
   strcpy(color, "None");
  }
  DomesticAnimal(int aWeight, float aPrice, char *aColor)
  {
   weight = aWeight;
   price = aPrice;
   strcpy(color, aColor);
  }
  virtual void print(void)
  {
   cout << "The weight = " << weight << "\n";
   cout << "The price = $" << price << "\n";
   cout << "The color = " << color << "\n";
  }
};

class Cow : public DomesticAnimal
{
 public:
  Cow(int aWeight, float aPrice, char *aColor)
    : DomesticAnimal(aWeight, aPrice, aColor) {}
  void print(void)
  {
   cout << "The cow has the properties:\n";
   DomesticAnimal::print();
  }
};

class Buffalo : public DomesticAnimal
{
 public:
  Buffalo(int aWeight, float aPrice, char *aColor)
    : DomesticAnimal(aWeight, aPrice, aColor) {};
  void print(void)
  {
   cout << "The buffalo has the properties:\n";
   DomesticAnimal::print();
  }
};
```

```
class Beefalo : public DomesticAnimal
{
 public:
  Beefalo(int aWeight, float aPrice, char *aColor)
   : DomesticAnimal(aWeight, aPrice, aColor) {}
   void print()
   {
    cout << "The beefalo has the properties:\n";
    DomesticAnimal::print();
   }
};
```

In addition to revising the inheritance relationships, Listing 9.12 improves on Listing 9.11 in three less significant ways that make the program easier to read and also a little more efficient. First, the derived constructors do not initialize the base protected data members directly. In the original code these data members were initialized twice, once by a base constructor and then again by a derived constructor. The derived constructors now simply pass their arguments back to the base constructor, so only one constructor executes per object. Second, the reason that data members were protected was to permit access from derived constructors. Because the derived constructors no longer assign values to them, the base data members can now be private, improving the encapsulation of DomesticAnimal. Third, the default constructors for Cow and Buffalo have been removed. The default constructors were needed only for the multiple inheritance. Because Cow and Buffalo were base classes of Beefalo, the Beefalo constructor was obliged to initialize both Cow and Buffalo unless a default constructor was present. Beefalo does not have a default constructor. Why should Cow or Buffalo, now that they are no longer base classes?

Figure 9.7 Revised DomesticAnimal inheritance hierarchy

The original `Beefalo` class is the result of a common misunderstanding about an important difference between biological inheritance and class inheritance in C++. Biological offspring "inherit" traits from both parents, but that does not mean that class inheritance is a good way to model the relationship in software. Using inheritance to model procreation requires that each object be of a class that is instantiated only once. Chapter 1 demonstrated the weakness of this approach to building programs, captured in the rule:

> ▶ **A class should describe a set of objects.**

A better model of biological inheritance is that each species is a class, and each animal is an object instantiated from the species class. An offspring object is initialized by receiving genetic information, a value, that is a combination of the genetic values of its parent objects. When modelled in software, biological inheritance is a relationship between objects, not classes.

Multiple Protocol Inheritance

There is a special situation in which multiple inheritance does appear to be useful. Ideally, its merit would be demonstrated by finding a program that is improved by rethinking its design to exploit multiple inheritance. I have encountered no such programs and, therefore, simply present a plausible example of multiple inheritance in isolation. (The selection criteria applied elsewhere in the book prohibit the creation of an artificial program to serve as a straw man.)

The problem is to create a `Clock` class similar in some respects to the `Monitor` class from earlier in the chapter. Each `Clock` object is to maintain the time of day in a window on a multi-window terminal. The `Clock` class is to be implemented in terms of a `Timer` class and a `Window` class. The `Timer` class and an auxiliary `TimerClient` class are declared as follows:

```
class TimerClient
{
public:
virtual void tick() = 0;
virtual      ~TimerClient() {}
};

class Timer
{
```

```
        // ...

public:
            Timer(int period, TimerClient *client);
            ~Timer();
};
```

At its creation, a `Timer` object is given a period (in seconds, say) and the identity of a `TimerClient` object. The `TimerClient` class is an abstract base class that establishes a *callback protocol* by which a `Timer` object communicates with its client. Cycling at the specified period, the `Timer` object repeatedly calls the `tick()` member function of its client. The `Timer` object knows only that its client satisfies the `TimerClient` interface.

This naive `Window` class and its auxiliary callback protocol class are

```
class WindowClient
{
public:
virtual void refresh() = 0;
virtual      ~WindowClient() {};
};

class Window
{

    // ...

public:
        Window(WindowClient *client);
        ~Window();
    void write(const char *text);
};
```

A client of a `Window` object can display text in the window by calling `Window::write` with a character string argument. The client calls `write` when it needs to change the text displayed in the window. However, the `Window` object must also be able to communicate with its client in the event that the window is "damaged" by unrelated activity on the screen. Typically, damage results from another window that is positioned "in front" of the client's window; when the other window is removed, the client must be told to refresh the contents of its window. Damage refresh is the purpose of the `WindowClient` class. The `Window` constructor requires a pointer to a `WindowClient` object; a `Window` object calls `refresh()` to inform its client that the window's contents need to be refreshed.

A Clock object must be a client of both a Timer object and a Window object. For the Timer object, a Clock object must be a TimerClient, and for the Window object it must be a WindowClient. The dual role is obtained by declaring Clock to be a derived class of both TimerClient and WindowClient, as shown in Listing 9.13.

Listing 9.13 Class Clock

```
class Clock : public TimerClient, public WindowClient
{
    Timer    *timer;
    Window   *win;
    void     display();
public:
             Clock();
             ~Clock();
    void     tick();      // Timer callback
    void     refresh();   // Window callback
};

Clock::Clock()
{
    timer = new Timer(5, this);
    win = new Window(this);
    assert( timer != NULL && win != NULL );
}

Clock::~Clock()
{
    delete timer;
    delete win;
}

void Clock::tick()
{
    display();
}

void Clock::refresh()
{
    display();
}
```

```
void Clock::display()
{
    time_t time_of_day;
    time(&time_of_day);
    const int size = 128;
    char buffer[size];
    strftime(buffer, size, "%H:%M:%S", localtime(&time_of_day));
    win->write(buffer);
}
```

The `Clock` constructor creates both a `Timer` and a `Window` object. The first argument causes the `Timer` object to call `Clock::tick()` every five seconds. The `Window` object calls `Clock::refresh()` whenever the window is in need of repair. Both `tick()` and `refresh()` call `display()`, which formats the time of day as `hh:mm:ss` and writes the information to the window.

Note that the "is-a" relationships between `Clock` and its base classes are *not* motivated by natural abstractions from the problem domain. `TimerClient` and `WindowClient` are *synthetic abstractions* in the software solution domain. A `Clock` object is a client of both `Timer` and `Window`. The properties of `Clock` are constrained by the other objects with which it must interact in the software system. Fruitful uses of multiple inheritance are more likely to be found in this setting than in attempts to model multiple classifications of real-world abstractions. Also note that the multiple base classes are abstract base classes that carry no state. For such classes, the question of whether or not they are virtual base classes is moot; they have no state to replicate.

Summary

Multiple inheritance in C++ is complicated and difficult to use effectively. Consensus on which parts of multiple inheritance are useful, and in which contexts, had yet to emerge within the community of C++ programmers at the time of this writing. The reader who has mastered the semantics of multiple inheritance should experiment with its use. Go beyond the drawing of inheritance graphs. The subtle interactions are best seen by writing the corresponding classes and using them from within client code. Do not stop with the first arrangement of classes that emerges; try a variety of class relationships to see which work.

Bibliographic Notes

For further discussion of multiple inheritance in C++, see Coplien [1] or Meyers [3]. Coplien makes a distinction between "static" and "dynamic" multiple inheritance; Meyers studies several sample programs.

1. Coplien, J. 1992. *Advanced C++ Programming Styles and Idioms*. Reading, MA: Addison-Wesley.

2. Ellis, M. A. and Stroustrup, B. 1990. *The Annotated C++ Reference Manual*. Reading, MA: Addison-Wesley.

3. Meyers, S. 1992. *Effective C++*. Reading, MA: Addison-Wesley.

Exercises

9.1. The program in Listing 9.14 has a virtual base class with a default constructor, a copy constructor and an assignment operator. The derived classes have compiler-supplied constructors and assignment operators. When the

```
copy = first;
```

assignment is executed in `main()`, how many times should `Top::operator=` be called? How does your compiler handle this program?

Listing 9.14 Exercise 9.1

```
class Top {
    int     x;
public:
            Top();
            Top(const Top &);
    Top & operator=(const Top &);
};

Top::Top() : x(0)
{
    cout << "\tTop::Top() this=" << this << "\n";
}

Top::Top(const Top & t) : x(t.x)
{
    cout << "\tTop::Top(const Top &) this=" << this << "\n";
}
```

```
Top & Top::operator=(const Top & rhs)
{
    cout << "\tTop::operator=() this=" << this << "\n";
    if( this != &rhs )
        x = rhs.x;
    return *this;
}

class Left : public virtual Top {
    int y;
    // ...
};

class Right : public virtual Top {
    int z;
    // ...
};

class Bottom : public Left, public Right {
    // ...
};

int main()
{
    cout << "Bottom first;\n";
    Bottom first;
    cout << "Bottom copy = first;\n";
    Bottom copy = first;
    cout << "copy = first;\n";
    copy = first;
    return 0;
}
```

9.2. Can the virtual function be removed from class `DomesticAnimal` in Listing 9.12?

9.3. Suppose that class `Clock` in Listing 9.13 must maintain an image in two windows? If it creates two `Window` objects, how can it tell which `Window` object is calling its `refresh()` function?

10

Summary of Rules

This summary provides a review of each chapter by enumerating the rules as they appeared. Note that some rules are mentioned in more than one chapter.

Chapter 1: Abstraction

- Concentrate common abstractions in a base class.
- A class should describe a set of objects.
- Use data members for variation in value; reserve virtual functions for variation in behavior.
- A public derived class should be a specialization of its base class.
- Polymorphism is not the solution to every programming problem.

Chapter 2: Consistency

- A constructor should put its object in a well-defined state.
- Consider default arguments as an alternative to function overloading.
- Define object states consistently — identify class invariants.
- Define a class interface consistently — avoid surprises.
- Identify the `delete` for every `new`.
- Avoid computing and storing state information that is never used.

- When defining `operator=`, remember x = x.

- Replace repetitive expressions by calls to a common function.

Chapter 3: Unnecessary Inheritance

- Look for simple abstractions.

- Recognize inheritance for implementation; use a private base class or (preferably) a member object.

- Consider default arguments as an alternative to function overloading.

Chapter 4: Virtual Functions

- A derived class must treat inherited state consistently with its base class.

- If a public base class does not have a virtual destructor, no derived class nor members of a derived class should have a destructor.

- Usually, the destructor in a public base class should be virtual.

- Migrate common behavior to the base class.

- Reduce coupling — minimize interactions between classes.

- Use data members for variation in value; reserve virtual functions for variation in behavior.

- No class is perfect; too narrow a design is better than too broad.

- Consider default arguments as an alternative to function overloading.

Chapter 5: Operator Overloading

- Write clearly — don't be too clever.

- The meaning of an overloaded operator should be natural, not clever.

- An overloaded operator must interact appropriately with other operators.

- Overload operators consistently.

- A set of overloaded operators should be complete.

- When defining `operator=`, remember x = x.

- When overloading operators, avoid surprises.
- Recognize inheritance for implementation; use a private base class or (preferably) a member object.

Chapter 6: Wrappers

- Know the valid lifetime of a pointer returned from a function.
- Independent objects should have independent behavior.
- Do not encapsulate essential information — make it available by some means.
- The behavior of an object that has encountered an error should be well-defined.
- Make a C++ wrapper an improvement over the C interface.

Chapter 7: Efficiency

- Reduce coupling — minimize interactions between classes.
- Don't guess. Use an execution profiler to isolate performance problems.
- Look in class implementations for the source of performance problems.
- Look in client code for the source of performance problems.
- A complete interface invites efficient client code.
- Look for simple abstractions.

Chapter 8: A Case Study

- Remember the null byte — use `new char[strlen(s)+1]`.
- Don't use a constructor to initialize static data members.
- Reduce coupling — minimize interactions between classes.
- Each class should serve a single, coherent purpose.
- Design abstract data types rather than modules.
- Use data members for variation in value; reserve virtual functions for variation in behavior.

- Don't solve a specific case if the general case is as simple.

- Usually, the destructor in a public base class should be virtual.

Chapter 9: Multiple Inheritance

- Before using virtual base classes, understand them thoroughly.

- Do not try to learn the semantics of multiple inheritance from your compiler.

- Avoid artificially limiting a class to serve only as a base class.

- If a public base class does not have a virtual destructor, no derived class nor members of a derived class should have a destructor.

- If a multiple inheritance hierarchy has any destructors, every base class should have a virtual destructor.

- Use a member object, not inheritance, to include a server in a client object.

- A class should describe a set of objects.

Index